US Liaison Aircraft
in action

By Al Adcock
Color by Don Greer
Illustrated by David Gebhardt

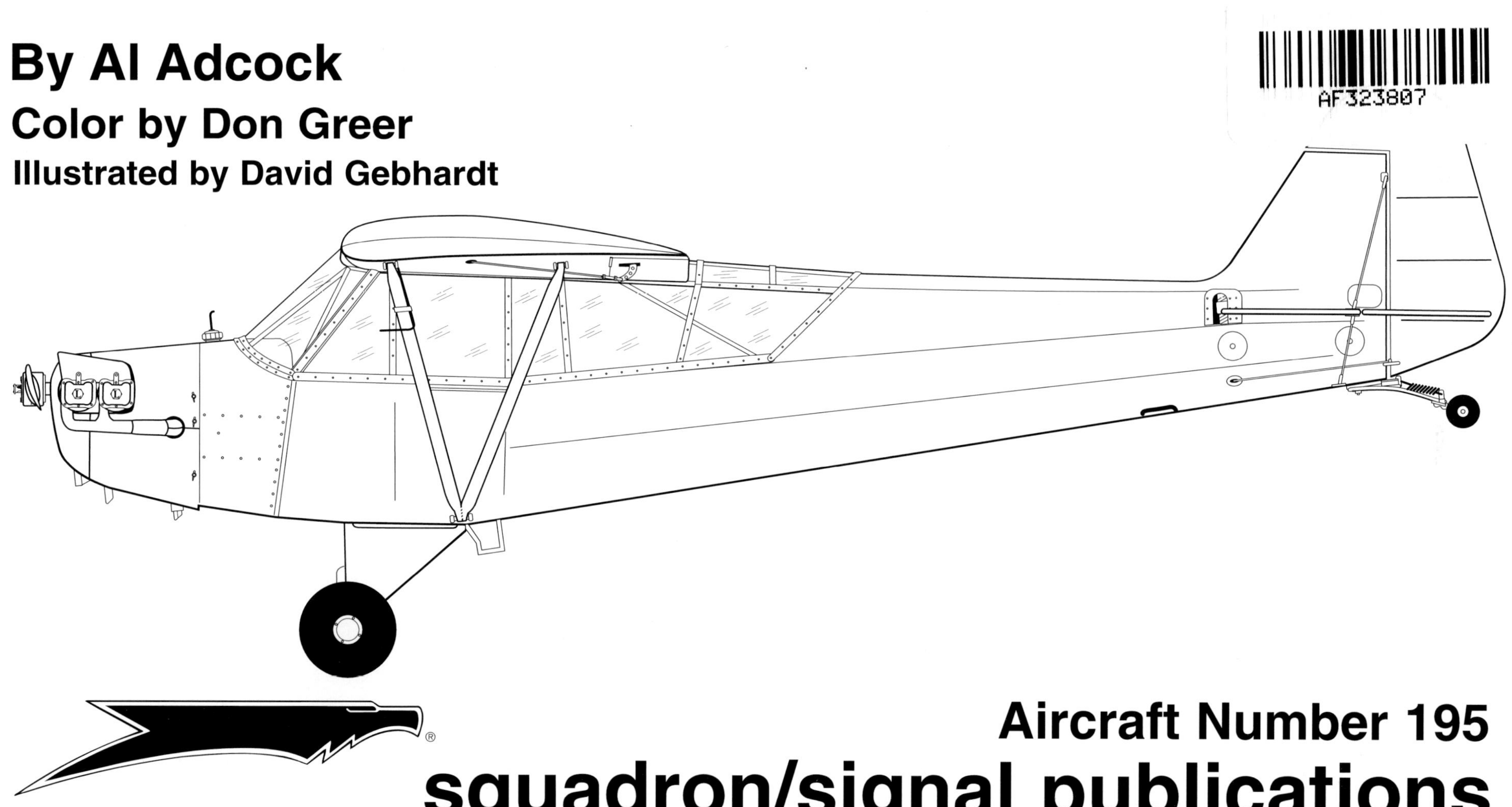

Aircraft Number 195

squadron/signal publications

A Piper L-4H-PI Grasshopper (39-F/43-29624) flies over Omaha Beach in Normandy, France just days after the Allied invasion of 6 June 1944 (Operation OVERLORD). This aircraft was assigned to the US Army V Corps Field Artillery, which employed it for observing and reporting on German positions. The L-4H-PI is camouflaged with Olive Drab 41 (ANA-613; FS34087) upper surfaces and Medium Green 42 (ANA-612; FS34092) splotches, with Neutral Gray 43 (FS36173) undersurfaces. Black and White 'Invasion' stripes are painted on the wings and fuselage.

Acknowledgements

US Army Aviation Museum
Richard Tierney
National Archives
Steve Dunn
US Army
US Navy
Real War Photos

Kim Chetwyn
Ed Gilmore
Terry Love
William T. Larkins
Squadron/Signal
  Publications
Garth C. Adcock

Paul S. Schmelzer
US Air Force (USAF)
Boardman C. Reed
US Marine Corps (USMC)
Frank J. Malmak
William E. Davis
Dave Ostrowski

Special Thanks:

To Terry Love for loaning me his extensive collection of 'L-Bird' photos; to Steve Dunn, Master Aircraft Restorer, for his expertise and advice on early light aircraft; and to Dick Tierney, US Army Aviation Museum, Fort Rucker, Alabama.

Author's Note:

Army/Navy Aircraft (ANA) color numbers were standardized in 1939 and are given where known. Federal Standard (FS) color numbers were developed after World War Two and are approximate.

ISBN 0-89747-487-2

If you have any photographs of aircraft, armor, soldiers or ships of any nation, particularly wartime snapshots, why not share them with us and help make Squadron/Signal's books all the more interesting and complete in the future. Any photograph sent to us will be copied and the original returned. The donor will be fully credited for any photos used. Please send them to:

Squadron/Signal Publications, Inc.
1115 Crowley Drive
Carrollton, TX 75011-5010

Если у вас есть фотографии самолётов, вооружения, солдат или кораблей любой страны, особенно, снимки времён войны, поделитесь с нами и помогите сделать новые книги издательства Эскадрон/Сигнал еще интереснее. Мы переснимем ваши фотографии и вернём оригиналы. Имена приславших снимки будут сопровождать все опубликованные фотографии. Пожалуйста, присылайте фотографии по адресу:

Squadron/Signal Publications, Inc.
1115 Crowley Drive
Carrollton, TX 75011-5010

軍用機、装甲車両、兵士、軍艦などの写真を所持しておられる方はいらっしゃいませんか？どの国のものでも結構です。作戦中に撮影されたものが特に良いのです。Squadron/Signal社の出版する刊行物において、このような写真は内容を一層充実し、興味深くすることができます。当方にお送り頂いた写真は、複写の後お返しいたします。出版物中に写真を使用した場合は、必ず提供者のお名前を明記させて頂きます。お写真は下記にご送付ください。

Squadron/Signal Publications, Inc.
1115 Crowley Drive
Carrollton, TX 75011-5010

The flight deck crew prepares a Piper L-4A Grasshopper (42-36389) named *Elizabeth* aboard the aircraft carrier USS RANGER (CV-4) on 8 November 1942. This occurred at the start of Operation TORCH, the Allied invasion of French North Africa. Lieutenant William Butler piloted the L-4A – also called a Cub – with Captain Brenton Devol as artillery spotter. Both the cowl and the ring around the fuselage national insignia were flat Orange-Yellow (ANA-614; FS33538). This mission marked the first time that the small US Army liaison aircraft entered combat. (US Navy)

Elizabeth
23

Introduction

The Wright Brothers – Orville and Wilbur – ushered in a new era when they made the first powered flight from the sands of Kitty Hawk, North Carolina on 17 December 1903. They thought that their little 'Flyer' would only be useful for carrying messages and for observation.

United States Army Aviation began when the Signal Corps took delivery of the world's first military aircraft, a Wright Model B two-place biplane pusher, on 2 August 1909. The aircraft cost $25,000 and met specifications that called for a maximum speed of 40 MPH (64 KMH), a range of 125 miles (201 KM), and could be easily controlled in all directions. This aircraft was rebuilt from the Wright A, which had crashed on 17 September 1908 and caused the first aircraft fatality. The Wright Model B was delivered to Fort Myer, Virginia for acceptance trials on 28 June 1909. Orville and Wilbur Wright went on to design and build many aircraft for the fledgling US Army Aviation before the beginning of World War One.

The second aircraft accepted by the US Army was the Curtiss Model D, designed by Glen Curtiss. This was also a two-place biplane pusher powered by a four-cylinder engine that produced 50 horsepower (HP) and had a speed of 50 MPH (80 KMH). Glen Curtiss produced many aircraft for both the military and civilian markets. Eugene Ely piloting one of Curtiss' 'flying machines' became the first man to fly off a ship in 1910.

US Army Aviation began to grow and over 500 aircraft from 14 builders had been ordered by 1917. The most widely produced of these aircraft was the Curtiss JN-4 'Jenny' with 93 delivered, mostly used as trainers. Other early names such as Glen L. Martin, Burgess, and Thomas also produced aircraft for the Signal Corps. There were no combat aircraft in the US Air Service inventory when the US entered the war in Europe on 6 April 1917. The Americans relied mainly on British and French aircraft. The Curtiss JN-4 and the de Havilland DH-4 were the most widely procured aircraft during this period, with over 10,000 produced by many American and Canadian aircraft companies.

The US Army Air Service procured various liaison and observation aircraft from 1919 through 1924. These included the Type VII Infantry Liaison (IL), Type IX Artillery Observation (AO) and Type X Corps Observation (CO) aircraft. All of these machines were biplanes except for the Engineering Division CO-1, which was a high-wing monoplane. The Air Service held a competition for a new observation aircraft in 1924. Contracts went to the Curtiss O-1 and Douglas O-2, both tandem seat biplanes powered by Curtiss and Liberty V-12 engines, respectively.

A successive string of observation aircraft were delivered to the US Army[1] after the O-1 and O-2 were accepted into service in 1924. Douglas, Curtiss, and Thomas Morse produced most of these aircraft. These ranged from the high-wing Douglas O-31 and O-43, plus the O-35 – the only twin-engine observation aircraft – to the Curtiss O-52 Owl and the North American O-47. The increasing size of observation aircraft made them more difficult to service in the field and their additional weight degraded their unimproved field performance. The US Army required a more efficient observation aircraft, which could operate in the field and be easily maintained. The 1938 National Air Races in Cleveland, Ohio provided the answer.

The German Air Force (*Luftwaffe*) was invited to display some of their aircraft at the air races and they were anxious to show off their Fieseler Fi 156 *Storch* (Stork) Short Take-Off and Landing (STOL) to the US and the world. The Fi 156 had won a *Reichsluftfahrtministerium* (RLM; German Aviation Ministry) competition for a STOL army co-operation aircraft in 1935. Fieseler's design beat out two other fixed-wing aircraft and an autogiro. The Fi 156 could takeoff in 213 feet (65 M) and land in 61 feet (19 M), plus it could hover in a 25 MPH (40 KMH) head wind. It caught the eye of various US Army aviators and generals and they expressed interest in building a Stork of their own.

[1]The US Army Air Service became the US Army Air Corps (USAAC) on 2 July 1926.

This was the initial Douglas O-38 (30-408). It was an improved O-25A airframe with a 525 HP Pratt & Whitney R-1690 Hornet radial engine replacing the 600 HP Curtiss V-1570 inline engine. The O-38 was armed with one .30 caliber (7.62MM) machine gun in the observer's position and four 100-pound (45 KG) bombs under the lower wing. Douglas built 45 O-38s for National Guard (NG) units in 1930 and 1931. (US Army)

This Douglas O-46A was one of 90 examples procured to replace the earlier O-38 during 1935. The O-46A featured a Direction Finding (DF) loop antenna on the lower fuselage and a fully enclosed cockpit. This aircraft had a Light Blue 23 (FS35109) fuselage and glossy Yellow 4 (FS13402) wing and tail surfaces. A 725 HP Pratt & Whitney R-1535 radial engine powered the O-46A. (US Army)

In 1939, the US Army issued a proposal that called for an Fi 156-type STOL aircraft. Twelve US aircraft manufacturers submitted ideas and proposals. The Army selected designs from Bellanca, Ryan, and Stinson and issued contracts for three prototype aircraft from these firms in 1940. These prototypes were built and then delivered to Wright Field, Ohio for testing. Bellanca Aircraft of New Castle, Delaware submitted a high-wing monoplane designated the **YO-50**. A 420 HP Ranger V-770 V-12 air-cooled engine powered it to a maximum speed of 125 MPH (201 KMH). The YO-50's 55-foot 6-inch (16.9 M) wingspan made it the largest of the three candidate aircraft.

Ryan Aeronautical of San Diego, California submitted the **YO-51 Dragonfly**, a high-wing monoplane with full width wing flaps that increased wing surface area for low-speed flight. It also had leading edge Handley Page slats, which were retracted during cruising flight and extended at high Angles of Attack (AoA). This slat diverted airflow over the wing at high AoA, which delayed stalling and allowed the aircraft to continue flight. The YO-51 was the only entrant with tandem open cockpits and it was the heaviest of the three finalists at 4206 pounds (1908 KG). A 440 HP Pratt & Whitney R-985-21 radial engine powered the YO-51 to a top speed of 130 MPH (209 KMH).

Stinson Aircraft of Fort Wayne, Indiana won the Army's 1940 competition. Their **Model 74** – Army designation **YO-49** – was a high-wing monoplane with drooping ailerons that drooped (lowered) 20° when the flaps were lowered. These ailerons increased lift while preserving lateral control. The YO-49 also had full span flaps and Handley Page leading edge slats. These features allowed the aircraft to take off and land in 200 feet (61 M). The US Army Air Corps awarded Stinson a production contract for 142 **O-49 Vigilant** observation aircraft in mid-1940.

The North American O-47 was a three-seat observation aircraft that entered US Army Air Corps (USAAC) service in 1937. A 975 HP Wright R-1820-49 radial engine powered this aircraft to a maximum speed of 221 MPH (356 KMH). This natural metal O-47 (1) was assigned to the 107th Observation Squadron (OS), Michigan NG at Wayne County Airport, Romulus, Michigan. (Paul C. Schmelzer)

The Fieseler *Storch*-like Ryan YO-51 Dragonfly (40-703) was the second of three designs entered in the US Army's STOL competition. The YO-51 featured full width flaps and leading edge slats on its 52-foot (15.9 M) wing and was powered by a 440 HP Pratt & Whitney R-985-21 radial engine. The Ryan design took off in less than 100 feet (30.5 M). (Via Terry Love)

The Bellanca YO-50 (40-741) was the first of three aircraft entered in the US Army's Short Take Off and Landing (STOL) aircraft contest in 1940. The YO-50 had a wingspan of 55 feet 6 inches (16.9 M) and a length of 35 feet 2 inches (10.7 M). A 425 HP Ranger V-770-1 air-cooled inline engine powered this aircraft. (Bellanca via Terry Love)

Development

Stinson L-1 (O-49) Vigilant

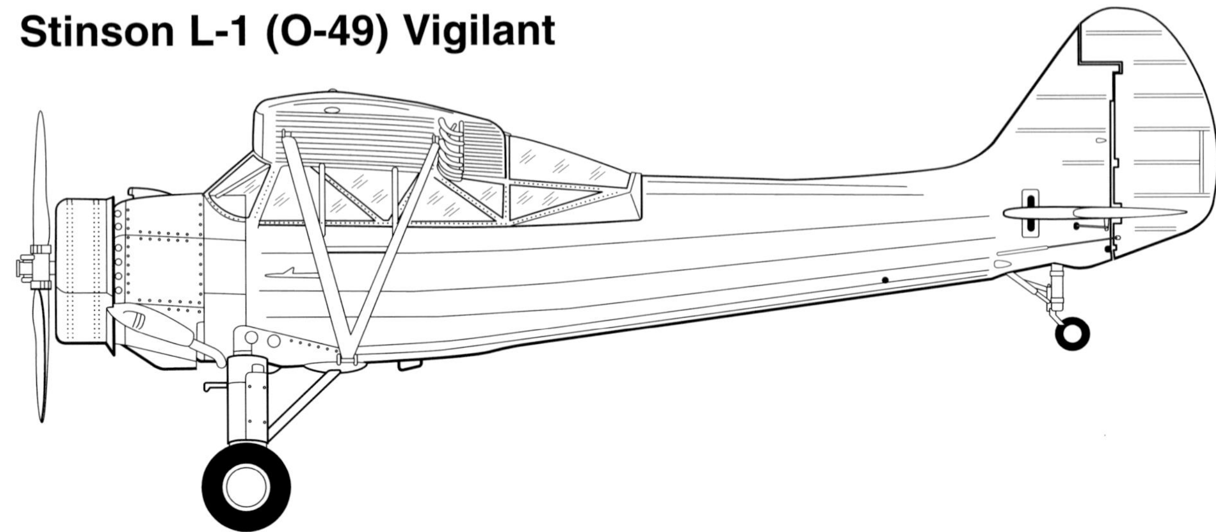

Taylorcraft L-2 (O-57) Grasshopper

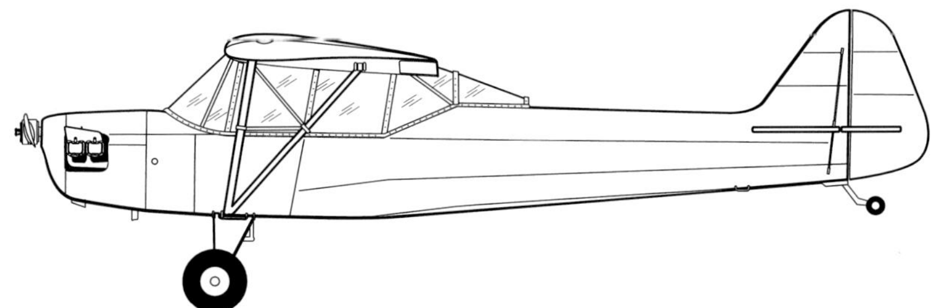

Piper L-4 (O-59) Grasshopper

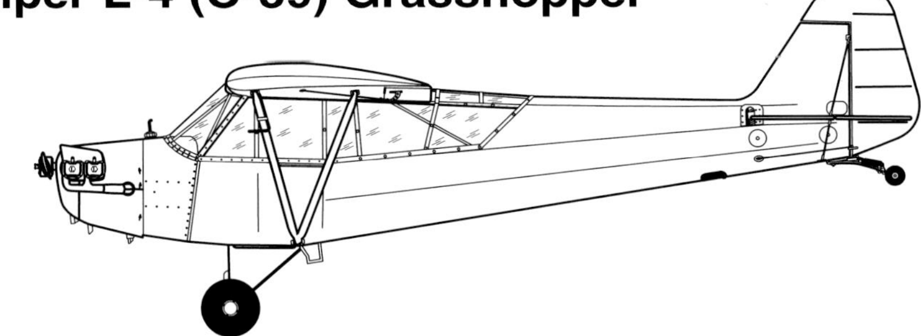

Aeronca L-3 (O-58) Grasshopper

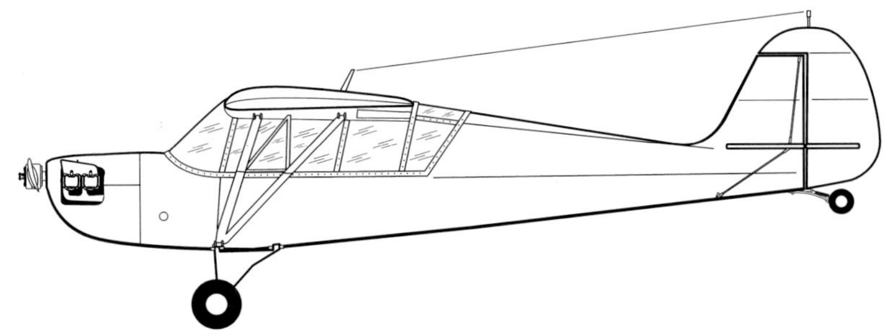

Stinson L-5 (O-62) Sentinel

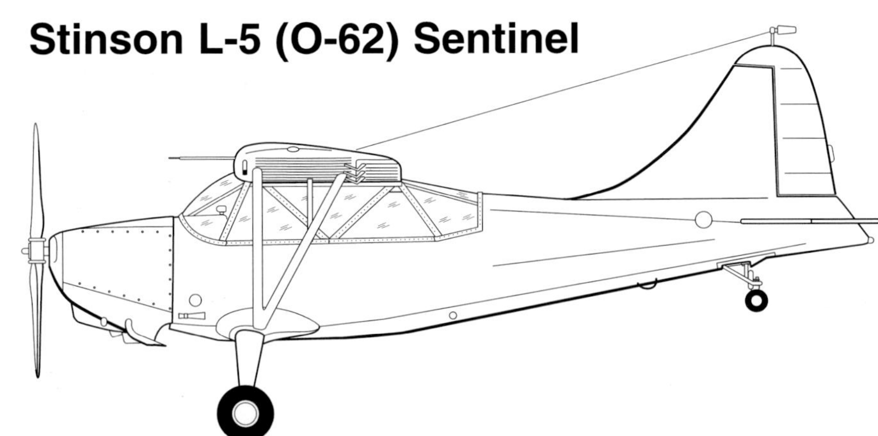

Stinson L-1 (O-49) Vigilant

Vultee Aircraft acquired Stinson Aircraft in the Summer of 1940, soon after the US Army Air Corps (USAAC) awarded Stinson the O-49 contract. Production began at Vultee's Nashville, Tennessee plant in the latter half of 1940.

The O-49 was a braced high-wing monoplane with a fixed landing gear. Doped fabric covered its metal tube framing, while aluminum skinning was used on the forward fuselage and cowling. The O-49 had a wingspan of 50 feet 11 inches (15.5 M), an overall length of 33 feet 2 inches (10.1 M), and a height of 10 feet 2 inches (3.1 M). Its empty weight was 2670 pounds (1211 KG) and its maximum take off weight was 3325 pounds (1508 KG). A 295 HP Lycoming R-680-9 nine-cylinder air-cooled radial engine turned a two-bladed constant-speed propeller.

The O-49 had a maximum speed of 129 MPH (208 KMH), an economical cruise speed of 95 MPH (153 KMH), and a stall speed of 35 MPH (56 KMH). Its service ceiling was 12,600 feet (3840 M) and its range was 280 miles (451 KM). The pilot and observer sat in tandem within a fully enclosed cockpit that offered excellent visibility. O-49s were originally finished in overall Aluminum (FS17178), but this scheme was replaced from early 1941 by Olive Drab 41 (ANA-613; FS34087) upper surfaces over Neutral Gray 43 (FS36173) undersurfaces.

In April of 1942, the US Army Air Forces (USAAF)[1] discontinued the O (for Observation) aircraft designation in favor of L (for Liaison). This resulted in the O-49's redesignation as the **L-1**. Stinson built 142 O-49s (serial numbers 40-192/291 and 40-3101/3142). The US supplied 16 O-49/L-1s to Great Britain under Lend-Lease. The Royal Air Force (RAF) designated them as **Vigilant Is**.

The **O-49A** was an improved O-49 with a 13-inch (33 CM) fuselage extension behind the wing root. This increased the overall length to 34 feet 3 inches (10.4 M). Additionally, gross weight increased to 3400 pounds (1542 KG). The O-49A could be fitted with two EDO Model 77 amphibious floats for waterborne operation. Each float had a retractable nose and main wheel for land operations. Stinson completed 182 O-49As (41-18900/19081), which were redesignated as **L-1As** in 1942. One O-49A was designated as **CQ-2** and used to remotely control aerial targets. The US sent 55 O-49A/L-1As to Great Britain, which designated them **Vigilant IAs**.

Four O-49s were converted to ambulance duties and designated as **O-49Bs**. This conversion included modifying the right fuselage side behind the wing root by removing the glazing and adding a fold down door to receive a litter. The O-49B was designated the **L-1B** in 1942.

The single **L-1C** was an L-1A modified with a rear fuselage loading hatch and a cabin modified to accept a litter. This aircraft later received EDO Model 77 floats and was redesignated as L-1F. Eventually, Stinson converted 113 L-1Cs, which retained their original designation.

The **L-1D** was the designation for 21 L-1As that were converted for glider pickup training duties. A tow cable apparatus was installed under the rear fuselage. L-1Ds towed Aeronca **TG-5**, Taylorcraft **TG-6**, and Piper **TG-8** training gliders.

Seven L-1 ambulance conversions were designated as **L-1Es** when they were fitted with EDO Model 77 floats. The USAAF deployed most L-1Es to the China-Burma-India (CBI) Theater of Operations from 1943 to 1945.

The last O-49/L-1 variant was the **L-1F**, which was the 113 L-1C aircraft fitted with EDO Model 77 amphibious floats. Stinson built 324 O-49/L-1 aircraft from 1940 until 1941. These aircraft saw extensive service throughout World War Two, although their liaison work was taken over by later and smaller liaison aircraft.

[1] The US Army Air Corps (USAAC) became the US Army Air Forces (USAAF) on 20 June 1941.

The first production O-49 Vigilant (40-192) sits on Stinson's Nashville, Tennessee ramp following its roll out in 1940. This aircraft had a 50-foot 11-inch (15.5 M) wingspan and a gross weight of 3325 pounds (1508 KG). Those dimensions made the O-49 the smallest and lightest of the three entrants in the US Army's new observation aircraft competition. The O-49 beat out the Bellanca YO-50 and Ryan YO-51 to win the contest. (US Army)

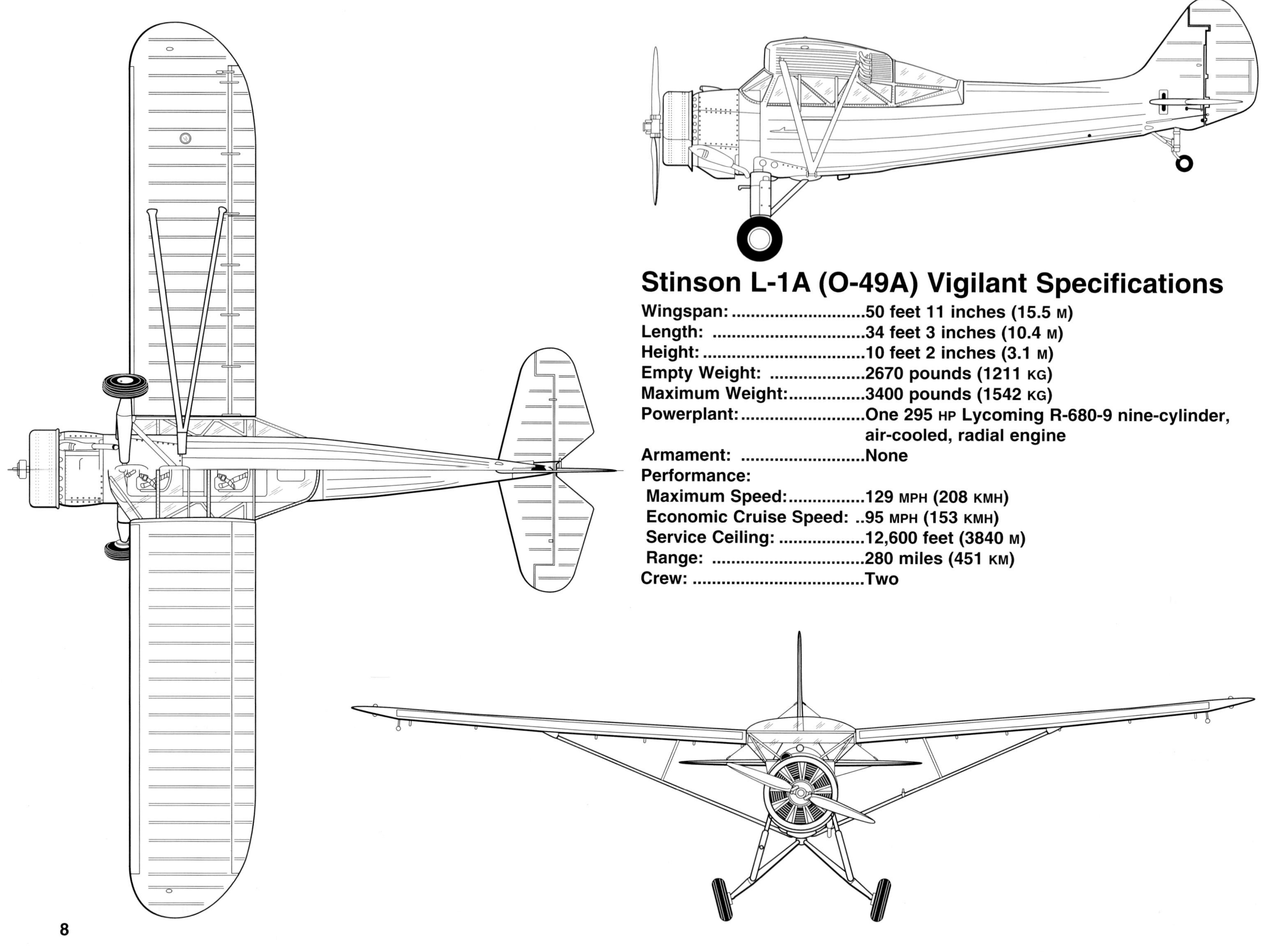

Stinson L-1A (O-49A) Vigilant Specifications

Wingspan: ....50 feet 11 inches (15.5 M)
Length: ....34 feet 3 inches (10.4 M)
Height: ....10 feet 2 inches (3.1 M)
Empty Weight: ....2670 pounds (1211 KG)
Maximum Weight:................3400 pounds (1542 KG)
Powerplant:.........................One 295 HP Lycoming R-680-9 nine-cylinder, air-cooled, radial engine
Armament: ....None
Performance:
 Maximum Speed:................129 MPH (208 KMH)
 Economic Cruise Speed: ..95 MPH (153 KMH)
 Service Ceiling: ....12,600 feet (3840 M)
 Range: ....280 miles (451 KM)
Crew: ....Two

(Above) An O-49 Vigilant demonstrates its slow speed flight ability on a test flight. The leading edge Handley Page slats are fully deployed. A flat Bronze Green 9 (FS34050) anti-glare panel was painted on the fuselage and cowl and the fuselage and wings are overall Aluminum (FS17178) dope. The rudder has seven Flag Red 15 (FS11105) and six White 25 (FS37778) horizontal stripes, with a Flag Blue 24 (FS15044) vertical stripe. (William T. Larkins)

(Above Right) An O-49 Vigilant sits on the ramp awaiting another test flight in 1940. A 295 HP Lycoming R-680-9 nine-cylinder radial air-cooled engine turned a two-bladed constant speed propeller. The steel tube frame fuselage was covered with Aluminum doped fabric. The wings featured full width flaps and ailerons that 'drooped' (lowered) with the flaps. (US Army)

(Right) An O-49 undergoes maintenance at a western United States airfield in 1941. An Olive Drab 41 (ANA-613; FS34087) camouflaged North American O-47 is parked on the flight line's opposite side. The O-49 was a large aircraft and required work stands to perform many maintenance jobs. The national insignia is placed on the four upper and lower wing positions, with U.S. painted on the lower right wing and ARMY on the lower left wing. The U.S. ARMY title was in flat Black 44 (ANA-604; FS37038). (US Army)

(Above Left) The 111th Observation Squadron (OS) at Brownwood, Texas received its first O-49 in July of 1941. A North American BC-1A (later AT-6) basic combat trainer shares the flight line in the hot Texas sun. The two-place O-49 had a maximum speed of 129 MPH (208 KMH) and a range of 280 miles (451 KM). Stinson built 142 O-49s that were delivered to the US Army Air Corps (USAAC), which became the US Army Air Forces (USAAF) on 20 June 1941. (Via Terry Love)

(Above) A 220th OS O-49 (12) flies over the simulated battlefield during the Louisiana War Games in September of 1941. The O-49 proved its worth to Army Aviation during these exercises. The Vigilant is camouflaged with Olive Drab upper surfaces and Neutral Gray 43 (FS36173) undersurfaces. The national insignia now appears on the fuselage sides, while the rudder striping was deleted. The aircraft number 12 is painted in Black on both the cowl and the vertical tail, appearing over 220 on the tail. (Terry Love)

(Left) The right cockpit door is slightly opened on this O-49. The USAAF redesignated this aircraft as the L-1 in April of 1942. The carburetor air intake is mounted just forward of the windshield and the cowling covers the 295 HP Lycoming R-680-9 nine-cylinder air-cooled radial engine. The constant speed propeller is painted Black. A slightly feathered demarcation line separates the Olive Drab upper surface and the Neutral Gray undersurface finish. (Via Terry Love)

An O-49 assigned to the 220th OS flies along a Louisiana country road during the September 1941 War Games. National insignia were painted on the upper left and lower right wings. The Black code 22012 on the upper left wing indicated this O-49 was the 220th OS's 12th aircraft. Sunshades installed in the greenhouse protected the crew and aircraft interior from the sun's heat. (Via Terry Love)

The O-49A (L-1A) differed from the O-49 (L-1) in having a 13-inch (33 CM) extension to the fuselage just behind the wing. This O-49A (17/41-18952) was configured for ambulance service. A flat Bright Red (ANA-509; FS31136) cross is painted on a flat Insignia White (ANA-601; FS37880) square on the fuselage. This cross is just forward of the new national insignia adopted in May of 1942. Both the aircraft number on the cowl and the serial number on the tail are in Orange-Yellow. (US Army)

The British received 55 L-1As (ex-O-49As) under the Lend-Lease agreement and called them Vigilant IAs. This aircraft retains the US national insignia and Olive Drab over Neutral Gray camouflage, but has a British serial number (BZ126) painted on the aft fuselage. An individual aircraft number (53) is painted on the cowling in Orange-Yellow. The cowl rim is painted in either Red or Black. The propeller has a natural metal hub, flat Black blades, and Orange-Yellow blade tips. This Vigilant IA was modified to tow gliders. (US Army)

This L-1A Vigilant served in the China-Burma-India (CBI) Theater of Operations in 1944. Landing gear fairings were removed to lessen mud and other foreign debris build-up. Flaps and leading edge slats are deployed in anticipation of take off. The L-1A is camouflaged in Olive Drab over Neutral Gray, while the national insignia on the fuselage is the type adopted in September of 1943. (US Army)

This overall Aluminum L-1A (41-19031) was modified into an ambulance and equipped with skis for service in Alaska in 1944. The tail, cowl, and wing outer panels are painted flat Bright Red for recognition purposes in case the aircraft went down in the snow or tundra. The L-1A had a 13-inch (33 cm) fuselage extension and a higher gross weight than the earlier L-1. (US Army)

An L-1A (41-18918) lands near Remagen, Germany on 21 May 1945. This was two weeks after Germany surrendered to end World War Two in Europe. The overall Aluminum Vigilant has a Bright Red cross painted on the mid-fuselage. This marking indicated this L-1A's employment on medical evacuation (medevac) duties. The Vigilant's size made it too large for most liaison missions, which were flown by smaller aircraft. (USAF)

An overall Aluminum O-49B warms up its Lycoming R-680-9 radial engine at Moffett Field, California on 6 December 1941 – one day before the Japanese attacked Pearl Harbor, Hawaii. This Vigilant was one of four O-49s converted into aerial ambulances. The litter section is located below the right wing root. A Bright Red cross painted on the fuselage distinguished this aircraft as an ambulance. The US national insignia was painted on four wing stations per regulations. The USAAF redesignated the O-49B as the L-1B in April of 1942. (William T. Larkins)

The sole L-1C (formerly O-49C) was a single L-1A modified for the ambulance role. A loading hatch replaced the upper fuselage observer's canopy and the rear cockpit was modified to accept a patient on a litter. Landing gear fairings were removed to facilitate flying from rough and muddy terrain. The overall Aluminum Vigilant has a Bright Red cowling and aft fuselage cross. This L-1C was later converted to be an L-1F amphibian, but 113 other L-1As were modified to L-1C standard. (US Army)

An L-1E-ST on amphibian EDO Model 77 floats and an L-1A share the flight line at Myogan Airfield, Burma in 1944. The L-1E was one of seven built and it appears to be camouflaged in Olive Drab over Aluminum dope. Its two floats featured retractable wheels, which enabled the L-1E to operate from either land or water. Stinson converted 113 L-1Cs to L-1F amphibian standard. (USAF via Terry Love)

An L-1D is parked on the flight line at an unidentified US Army glider training base located in the southwest United States in 1943. This Vigilant was one of 21 L-1As converted for glider pick up training. The L-1D is finished in Olive Drab upper surfaces over Neutral Gray under-surfaces. Silver doped Taylorcraft TG-6 gliders – derivatives of the L-2 Grasshopper – are lined up awaiting their students and instructors. (Via Terry Love)

L-1F Floatplane

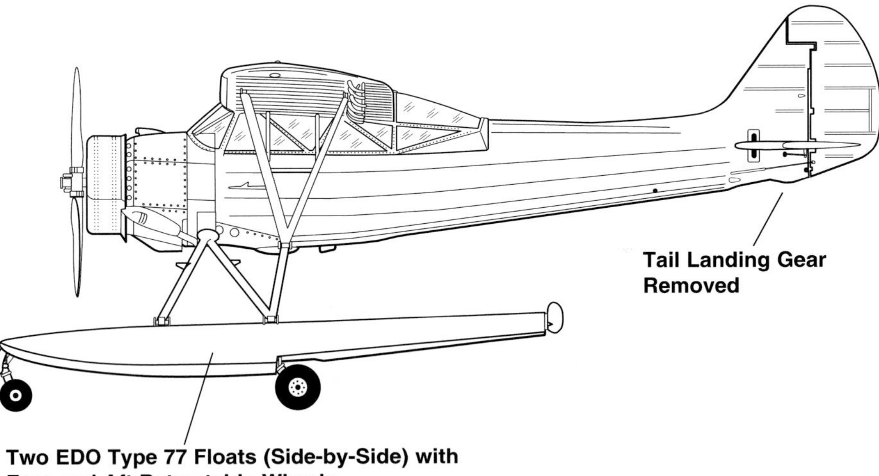

Taylorcraft L-2 (O-57) Grasshopper

On 2 June 1941, the US Army requested three manufacturers – Taylorcraft, Aeronca, and Piper – to each provide four light aircraft. These aircraft were to be evaluated during maneuvers being held in mid to late 1941. The Taylorcraft Aviation Company of Alliance, Ohio responded with their **Model DC-65**, a high-wing monoplane tandem-seat trainer. These aircraft were each fitted with a radio and painted Olive Drab over Neutral Gray with US Army Air Forces (USAAF) markings. The DC-65 received the USAAF designation **YO-57**.

The YO-57 had a fabric-covered metal tube structure and a fixed landing gear. It had a wingspan of 35 feet 5 inches (10.8 M), a length of 22 feet 9 inches (6.9 M), and a height of 6 feet 8 inches (2 M). Its empty weight was 680 pounds (308 KG) and the maximum takeoff weight was rated at 1200 pounds (544 KG). Its 65 HP Continental YO-170-3 four-cylinder, air-cooled, horizontally-opposed ('flat') engine turned a two-bladed wooden fixed-pitch propeller. This engine gave the aircraft a maximum speed of 93 MPH (150 KMH). The YO-57's range was 230 miles (370 KM) with the 18-gallon (68.1 L) maximum fuel capacity. The US Army purchased four YO-57s (serial numbers 42-452/455) under a contract worth $13,888 and deliveries were made on 11 September 1941. In 1942 the four YO-57s were redesignated as **L-2s**.

Following field evaluations, a follow-on contract was signed for 20 additional aircraft (42-7773/7792) designated **O-57s**. The O-57 was essentially a YO-57 with a production standard 65 HP Continental O-170-3 engine. A contract for 50 more O-57s (43-2859/2908) soon followed. These aircraft entered service as **L-2-TAs** in 1942. (TA was the USAAF code for Taylorcraft.) By this time, the O-57 and other light observation aircraft were dubbed 'Grasshoppers' for their ability to take off and land from the unimproved grass airfields.

In 1942 Taylorcraft introduced a modified version of the O-57 that featured a cut down turtle deck. This was the area between the after wing root and the base of the horizontal stabilizer. The reduced turtle deck improved visibility to the top, side, and rear. This variant was also equipped with an observer's seat that could rotate 180° and an SCR-585 radio. The new Grasshopper was originally designated the O-57A, but the 336 aircraft ordered (42-15073/15158 and 42-35825/36074) entered USAAF service as **L-2As**. Taylorcraft built 140 more aircraft (42-38498/38537 and 43-25754/25853) designated as **L-2A-TAs**.

The 490 **L-2B-TAs** (43-001/490) were L-2As modified for the US Army Field Artillery. These aircraft had additional equipment for artillery spotting, including range finders. The USAAF impressed 52 civilian models for training duties. These included 13 **Model DC65s (L-2Cs)**, one **Model DL65 (L-2D)**, ten **Model DP65s (L-2Es)**, seven **Model BL65s (L-2Fs)**, two **Model BFT65s (L-2Gs)**, nine **Model BC12-65s (L-2Hs)**, five **Model BL12-65s (L-2Js)**, four **Model BF12-65s (L-2Ks)**, and one **Model BF50 (L-2L)**.

The **L-2M-TA** was a modified L-2B with a fully enclosed close fitting engine cowling and wing spoilers to improve short field landings. Additionally, standard USAAF instruments were fitted along with improved radios for air-to-ground communications. Taylorcraft built 900 L-2Ms (43-25854/26753), which brought total O-57/L-2 production to 1800 aircraft (including the four YO-57s) by 1943.

Taylorcraft's **Model ST.100** was an unpowered O-57/L-2 glider version, which the USAAF designated as the **TG-6**. This was a much-modified Model D civilian trainer whose engine and fuel system were removed. An enlarged nose accommodated an instructor and two students under an expanded greenhouse. This increased the TG-6's length to 25 feet 2 inches (7.7 M) – 2 feet 5 inches (0.7 M) longer than the L-2. Additionally, the lengthened nose compensated for the engine's lost weight and preserved the glider's weight and balance. Further modifications included an enlarged vertical stabilizer and shortened main landing gear struts. The TG-6 uti-

The prototype Taylorcraft YO-57 (42-452) is parked at Wright Field, Dayton, Ohio during testing in 1941. The O-57 was redesignated the L-2 in April of 1942, but the Grasshopper nickname was retained. A 65 HP Continental YO-170-3 four-cylinder air-cooled engine powered the YO-57 to a maximum speed of 93 MPH (150 KMH). (US Army)

The antenna wire drogue atop the YO-57's vertical stabilizer indicated that a radio was installed on this aircraft. The Grasshopper is camouflaged in Olive Drab over Neutral Gray, with the US national insignia in four positions (upper and lower left and right wings). U.S. ARMY is painted in Black across the lower wing surfaces. The O-57 weighed 1200 pounds (544 KG) when fully loaded. (US Army)

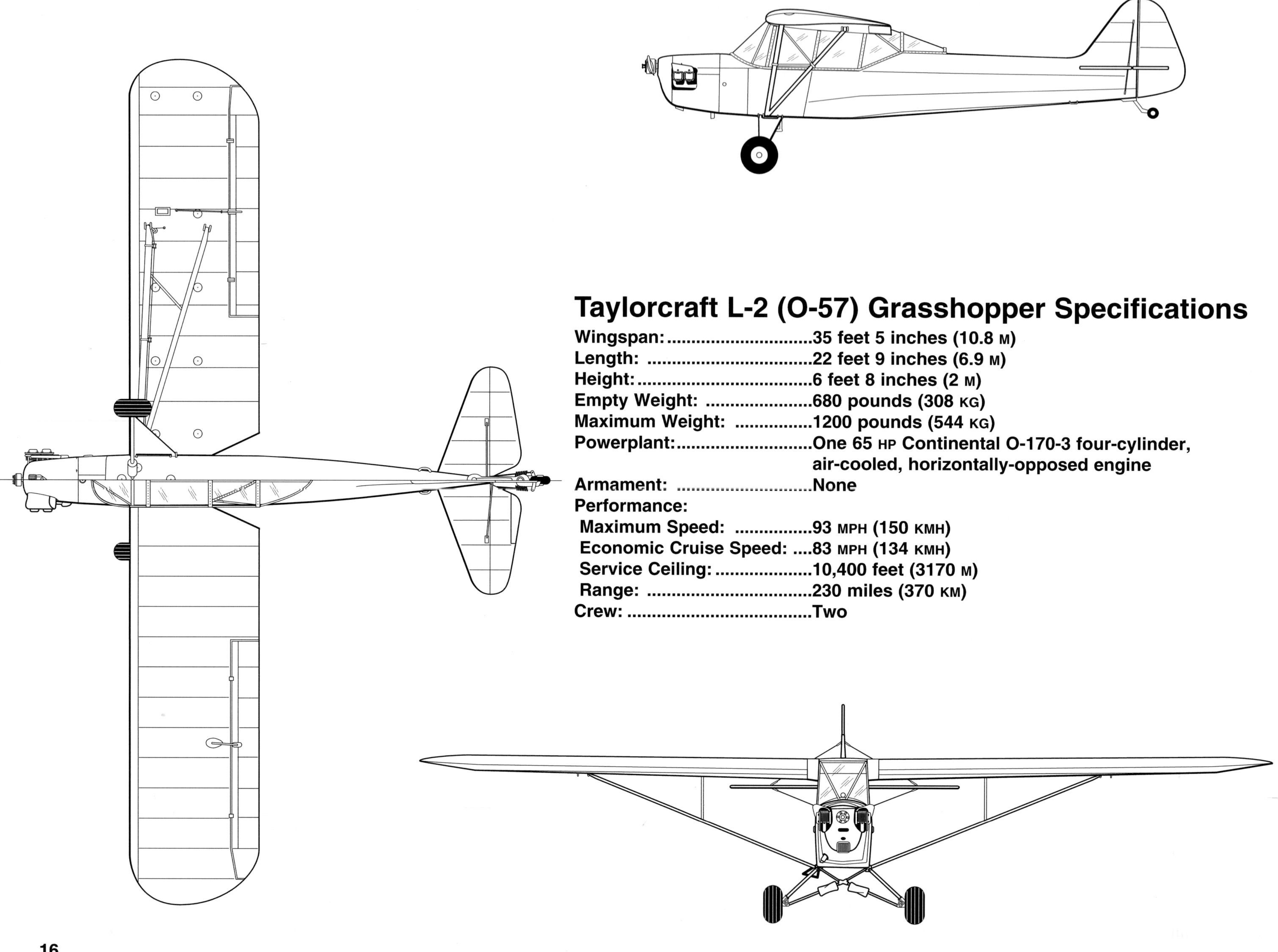

Taylorcraft L-2 (O-57) Grasshopper Specifications

Wingspan: ....35 feet 5 inches (10.8 M)
Length: ....22 feet 9 inches (6.9 M)
Height: ....6 feet 8 inches (2 M)
Empty Weight: ....680 pounds (308 KG)
Maximum Weight: ....1200 pounds (544 KG)
Powerplant:...........................One 65 HP Continental O-170-3 four-cylinder,
                                                    air-cooled, horizontally-opposed engine
Armament: ....None
Performance:
 Maximum Speed: ....93 MPH (150 KMH)
 Economic Cruise Speed: ....83 MPH (134 KMH)
 Service Ceiling: ....10,400 feet (3170 M)
 Range: ....230 miles (370 KM)
Crew: ....Two

The L-2A differed from the O-57 (L-2) in having a cut down rear fuselage and having the glass extended along its upper area. This increased visibility for the observer seated in the aft cockpit. A 65 HP Continental O-170-3 turned a Sensenich fixed-pitch wooden propeller. The 18-gallon (68.1 L) fuel capacity allowed for an operating range of 230 miles (370 KM). (US Army)

lized the L-2's wings, with upper and lower spoilers added for increasing the descent rate. TG-6s trained pilots that flew the Waco CG-4s used in the Allied invasion of France on 6 June 1944 (D-Day). These gliders were also used to determine the fledgling aviators' flying ability. Stinson L-1D-STs usually towed the TG-6s into the air. Taylorcraft built 250 TG-6 gliders in 1942. The USAAF 'bailed' (loaned) three TG-6s to the US Navy for evaluation in 1943, under the designation **XLNT-1**.

The Civilian Pilot Training Program (CPTP) used this Taylorcraft Model D – the L-2's civilian version – during World War Two. In early 1939, the Civil Aeronautics Authority (CAA) set up the CPTP to increase the number of trained pilots. The CPTP was renamed the War Training Service (WTS) in 1942 and the program was phased out in mid-1944. The Model D's fuselage was painted a Metallic Blue (approximate FS number unknown), with a Yellow fuselage stripe, wings, and horizontal stabilizer. The civilian registration number (39174) is painted in Yellow on the vertical stabilizer; the number's NC prefix was not painted. The registration number's last two digits (74) are painted on the lower left wing. (National Archives)

Taylorcraft produced 250 TG-6 training gliders for the US Army Air Forces (USAAF) during World War Two. This aircraft had an L-2 fuselage modified with a cabin for two students and a pilot instructor replacing the engine. Its wings were identical to those on the L-2, but with spoilers installed on the upper and lower surfaces. These spoilers increased the TG-6's descent rate to emulate that of the Waco CG-4 transport gliders that the students were training to fly. A fully laden TG-6 weighed 1100 pounds (499 KG). (National Archives)

One USAAF TG-6 fitted with tricycle landing gear became the prototype aircraft for the US Navy's LBT. It was envisioned that the LBT would carry an atomic bomb, which would be flown by remote control to its intended target. This project was soon dropped when the bomb's weight exceeded the glider's weight by ten fold. (US Army)

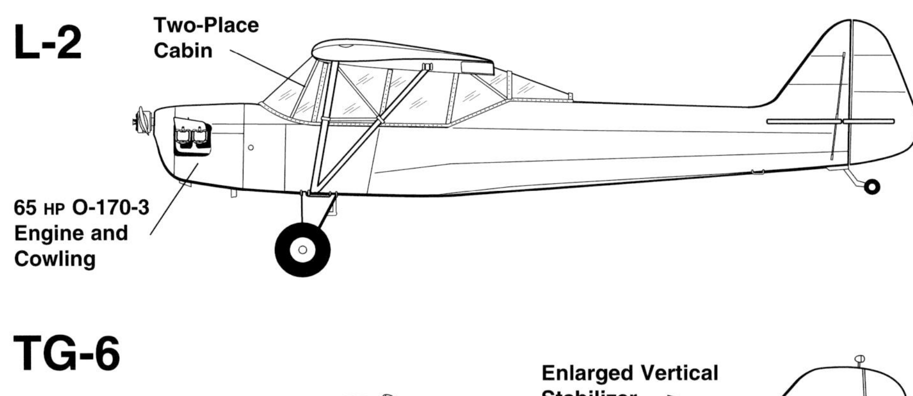

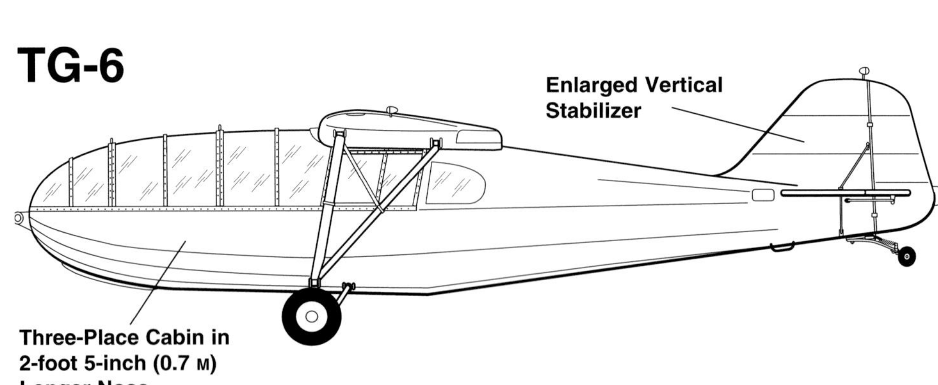

A US Army aviator leans up against an L-2A in early 1942. The Black wooden propeller has Orange-Yellow tips. A Red disc is located within the US national insignia's White star. This disc was removed in May of 1942 to prevent possible confusion with the Japanese *Hinomaru* national insignia. The officer wears an A-2 leather flight jacket and the obligatory Ray Ban sunglasses. (US Army)

This L-2A (Black 127) crashed during a low, slow landing approach at Fort Sill, Oklahoma in mid-1942. The accident killed the pilot, Lt. R.P. Stallings, who was the first fatality at the Fort's Artillery Spotting School. This Grasshopper was finished in overall Aluminum dope. Radio equipment enabled the L-2A's pilot to communicate with ground forces. (Via Terry Love)

Another overall Aluminum L-2A (Black 128) sits on the ramp between training missions. A Flat Black anti-glare panel is painted on the upper fuselage ahead of the windshield. This aircraft had a wingspan of 35 feet 5 inches (10.8 M), a length of 22 feet 9 inches (6.9 M), and an empty weight of 680 pounds (308 KG). Taylorcraft completed 476 L-2As for the USAAF at Alliance, Ohio during 1942. The L-2A was fitted with an SCR-585 radio and a swiveling rear seat that allowed the observer to face backwards. (US Army)

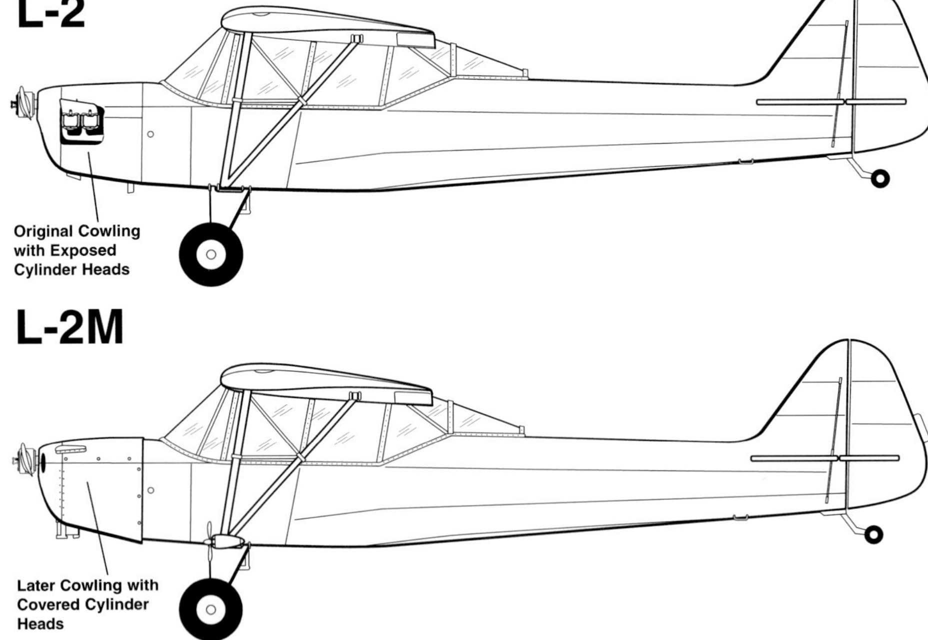

The L-2M was a basic L-2A with a close fitting cowling and wing spoilers. Taylorcraft built 900 L-2Ms – half the total L-2 production. This Grasshopper (43-26085) was camouflaged in Olive Drab upper surfaces over Neutral Gray undersurfaces. A small spinner is fitted to the natural wood propeller. The L-2M's rate of climb was 350 feet (107 м) per minute and it had a maximum speed of 98 MPH (158 кмн). (US Army)

An L-2M (B401/43-26235) named "KITTY" is tied down on a grass field somewhere in the United States on 6 September 1944. Orange-Yellow lettering and numbers are painted on the Olive Drab surfaces. A gust lock fitted to the rudder kept it from freely swinging in high winds. Canvas covers are placed over the windshield and observer's canopy. Another cover is fitted over the wooden propeller to protect it from the rain. An air driven generator mounted on the left wing strut provided electric power for the radio. (US Army via Squadron/Signal)

Aeronca L-3 (O-58) Grasshopper

The Aeronca Aircraft Company of Middletown, Ohio was the second of three manufacturers to provide light aircraft for US Army evaluation during the 1941 maneuvers. Following these tests, an $11,326 contract was issued for four **YO-58s** (42-456/459). This was the military version of Aeronca's **Model 65TC Defender** high-wing monoplane with the addition of a military radio and Olive Drab over Neutral Gray camouflage paint scheme.

The YO-58 was a braced high-wing monoplane with fixed landing gear. It had aluminum, steel tubing, and wood structure with a cloth covering. The YO-58 had a wingspan of 35 feet (10.7 M), a length of 21 feet 10 inches (6.7 M), and a height of 9 feet 1 inch (2.8 M). The empty weight was 835 pounds (379 KG) and the maximum takeoff weight was 1260 pounds (572 KG).

A 65 HP Continental YO-170-3 four-cylinder, air-cooled, horizontally-opposed engine turned a two-bladed wooden fixed-pitch propeller. This powerplant gave the YO-58 a maximum speed of 85 MPH (137 KMH). The aircraft had a service ceiling was 10,400 feet (3170 M) and its range was 230 miles (370 KM). Its two-man crew consisted of a pilot and observer sitting in tandem. No standard armament was fitted to this and other light observation aircraft; however, each crewman was usually issued with a .45 caliber (11MM) Colt M1911 pistol. Additionally, the crew was sometimes issued either a .45 caliber M3 submachine gun ('grease gun') or a .30 caliber (7.62MM) M1 carbine. The four YO-58s eventually became **O-58s** and then redesignated as **L-3s** in April of 1942.

In 1942, the US Army issued a follow-on contract for 50 additional O-58s (43-2809/2858). A production standard 65 HP Continental O-170-3 engine powered the O-58 and the only other change was the shape of the aft cabin side glass. The YO-58's trapezoid-shaped side windows were changed to oval-shaped windows. Most O-58s/L-3s were employed on stateside training duties during World War Two.

The **O-58A** was designed with a four-inch (10.2 CM) wider fuselage and a modified observer's window arrangement. These changes increased the maximum gross weight to 1350 pounds (612 KG). Aeronca built 20 O-58As (42-7793/7812), which were redesignated as **L-3As** in 1942.

The **O-58B** was based on the O-58A, but with a modified glass enclosure, additional radio equipment, and a gross take off weight raised to 1825 pounds (828 KG). Despite the increased weight, the maximum speed actually increased to 88 MPH (142 KMH). O-58B production totaled 335 aircraft (42-14713/14797 and 42-36075/36324). In 1942, the O-58B became the **L-3B**.

The **L-3C** was identical to the L-3B, except with no radio equipment fitted. Most L-3Cs went to the War Training Service (WTS) of the Civil Aeronautics Administration (CAA)[1] for basic flight training during World War Two. Aeronca built 490 L-3Cs (43-1471/1960) during 1943. The US Navy received three L-3Cs designated as **JR-1s** and stationed them at Brown Field, Naval Auxiliary Air Station (NAS) Otay Mesa, California. Aeronca completed 899 O-58/L-3 aircraft for the USAAF between 1941 and 1943.

The USAAF impressed 48 civilian models into service during World War Two. These included 11 **Model 65TF Defenders** (L-3Ds), 12 **Model 65TC Defenders** (L-3Es), 19 **Model 65CA Super Chiefs** (L-3Fs), four **Model 65L Super Chiefs** (L-3Gs), one **Model 65TL Defender** (L-3H), and one additional Model 65TC Defender (L-3J). These aircraft were used for training and 'hack' (utility) duties.

Aeronca designed and built a glider version of the L-3, which was designated the **TG-5**. The L-3's engine and fuel system were removed, while the fuselage and canopy were extended forward by 1 feet 9 inches (0.5 M) to accommodate a third crewmember. This increased the TG-5's length to 23 feet 7 inches (7.2 M). Additionally, the main landing gear was modified

[1]The Civil Aeronautics Administration (CAA) was established in 1940 to set up US air traffic control, airman and aircraft certification, safety enforcement, and airway development. The CAA was renamed the Federal Aviation Agency in 1958. In 1967, this agency was renamed the Federal Aviation Administration (FAA).

This YO-58 (42-456) was the first of four Aeronca 65TC Defenders built for the US Army in 1941. A White cross on the fuselage indicated its assignment to the White Force during the 1941 Louisiana Maneuvers. One 65 HP Continental YO-170-3 four-cylinder, air-cooled, horizontally-opposed engine powered the YO-58. An air driven generator between the main landing gear struts provided electrical power for the SRC-585 military radio. (US Army)

The US Army procured four YO-58 Grasshoppers for testing their feasibility in performing liaison missions, much as the Jeep did on the ground. The YO-58 had a wingspan of 35 feet (10.7 M) and a maximum gross weight of 1260 pounds (572 KG). A drogue atop the rudder pulled out the antenna wire to adjust the radio frequency. (US Army)

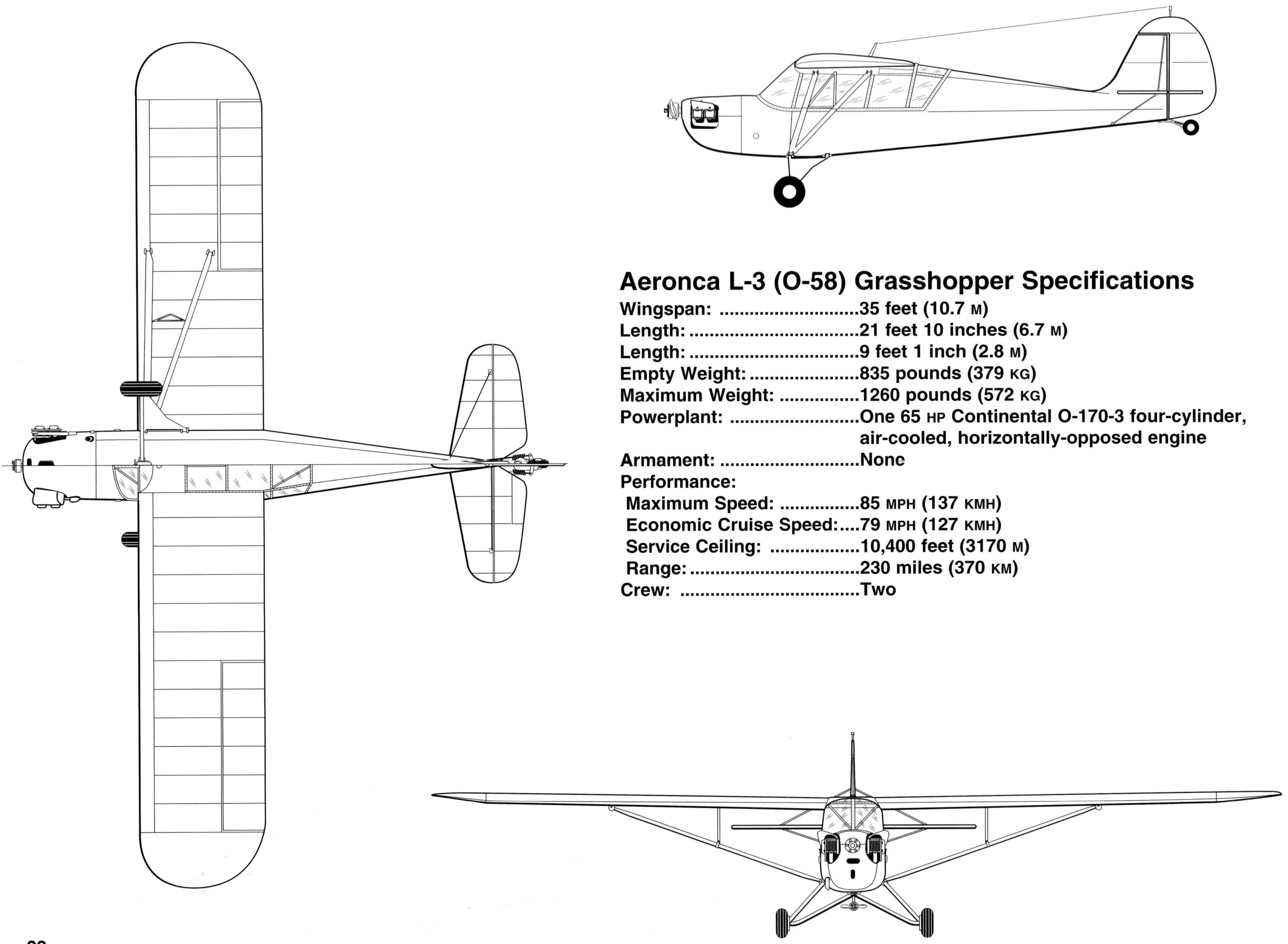

Aeronca L-3 (O-58) Grasshopper Specifications

Wingspan: ....35 feet (10.7 M)
Length: ....21 feet 10 inches (6.7 M)
Length: ....9 feet 1 inch (2.8 M)
Empty Weight: ....835 pounds (379 KG)
Maximum Weight: ....1260 pounds (572 KG)
Powerplant: ....One 65 HP Continental O-170-3 four-cylinder,
air-cooled, horizontally-opposed engine
Armament: ....None
Performance:
 Maximum Speed: ....85 MPH (137 KMH)
 Economic Cruise Speed:....79 MPH (127 KMH)
 Service Ceiling: ....10,400 feet (3170 M)
 Range: ....230 miles (370 KM)
Crew: ....Two

The first production O-58A (42-7793) makes a test flight over the Ohio landscape in early 1942. The O-58 (redesignated L-3A in April of 1942) could be flown from the front seat without an observer/passenger in the rear seat. An air-driven electrical generator is suspended from the center of the landing gear strut supports. A 65 HP Continental O-170-3 air-cooled engine powered this Grasshopper. (US Army)

from a Vee-type to a crossbar type and the vertical stabilizer was enlarged to increase stability. The USAAF used TG-5s for basic glider pilot training. Many of these students flew Waco CG-4 assault/cargo gliders during the 1944 invasion of Europe. Aeronca built 250 TG-5s, including three aircraft that were transferred to the US Navy under the designation **LNR** for evaluation.

Four engine instruments and two flight instruments are mounted on the L-3's instrument panel. The engine cylinder head temperature gauge is mounted at the far left, followed by (from left to right) the altimeter, airspeed indicator, voltmeter, engine Revolutions Per Minute (RPM) indicator, and oil pressure gauge. Sparse instrumentation meant the L-3 – like other US wartime liaison aircraft – flew under Visual Flight Rules (VFR). The control stick grip protrudes aft of and below the panel. (US Army)

L-3s, TG-5 training gliders, and Model 65 TC training aircraft crowd the factory floor at Aeronca's plant at Lunken Airport, Cincinnati, Ohio. Various wing panels wait mating to the fuselage during the assembly process. Aeronca built over 1700 light aircraft and training gliders from 1941 to 1945. Aeronca is a contraction of Aeronautical Corporation of America, the firm's original name. (US Army)

Most O-58/L-3 aircraft were used for training duties in the United States during World War Two. A few Grasshoppers reached units in the Pacific, European, and African theaters, but the more numerous Piper **L-4** soon superceded the L-3.

An L-3 named FLO (257/43-2823) accompanies some Waco CG-4 transport gliders during maneuvers in the US in 1944. It is believed this exercise was in training for the Allied invasion of France (Operation OVERLORD). The L-3 is camouflaged in Olive Drab upper surfaces and Neutral Gray undersurfaces, with markings in Orange-Yellow. Aeronca built 50 L-3s at its Cincinnati, Ohio factory. (US Army)

The prototype O-58B (42-14724) sits on the flight line at Aeronca's Ohio factory in early 1942. This variant featured a modified cockpit canopy and additional radio equipment. An air-driven electrical generator is suspended between the landing gear support struts. The O-58B (L-3B from April of 1942) is camouflaged in the standard Olive Drab 41 (ANA-613; FS34087) over Neutral Gray 43 (FS36173) scheme. The 65 HP Continental engine turned a wooden propeller painted Flat Black 44 (ANA-604; FS37038). (Via Terry Love)

An L–3B begins its take off roll on a test flight from the Aeronca factory airfield in 1942. The light colored vertical stabilizer panel contains aircraft information, including the US Army Air Forces (USAAF) serial number, construction date, Aeronca serial number, and engine serial number. The L-3B was usually fitted with an SRC-585 military radio and was primarily employed as a trainer. (US Army)

This L-3C (43-1925) rests on the flight line in late 1943. The L-3C was essentially the same as the L-3B, but no radio was installed. This variant retained the expanded observer's canopy introduced on the earlier L-3B. Aeronca produced 490 L-3Cs for the USAAF during a one-year period. (US Army via Terry Love)

The Stinson L-1F-ST was one of two Vigilant models equipped as ambulances and fitted with floats. This L-1F was painted in overall Aluminum (FS17178) Dope with a flat Bronze Green 9 (FS34050) anti-glare panel in 1940-41.

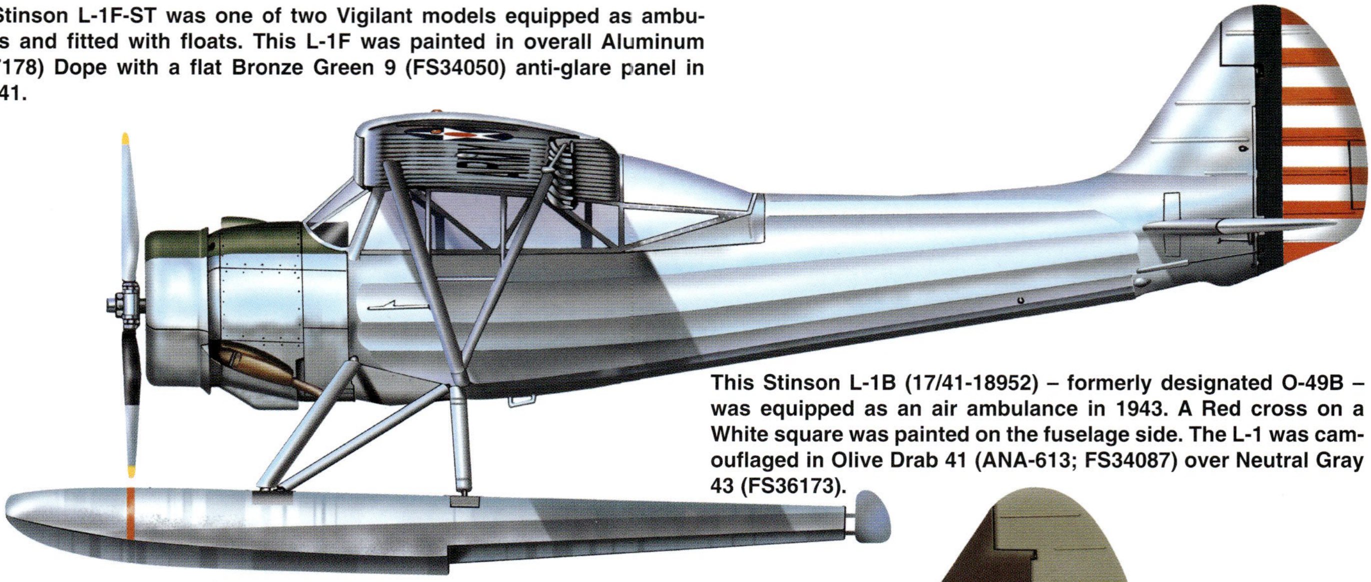

This Stinson L-1B (17/41-18952) – formerly designated O-49B – was equipped as an air ambulance in 1943. A Red cross on a White square was painted on the fuselage side. The L-1 was camouflaged in Olive Drab 41 (ANA-613; FS34087) over Neutral Gray 43 (FS36173).

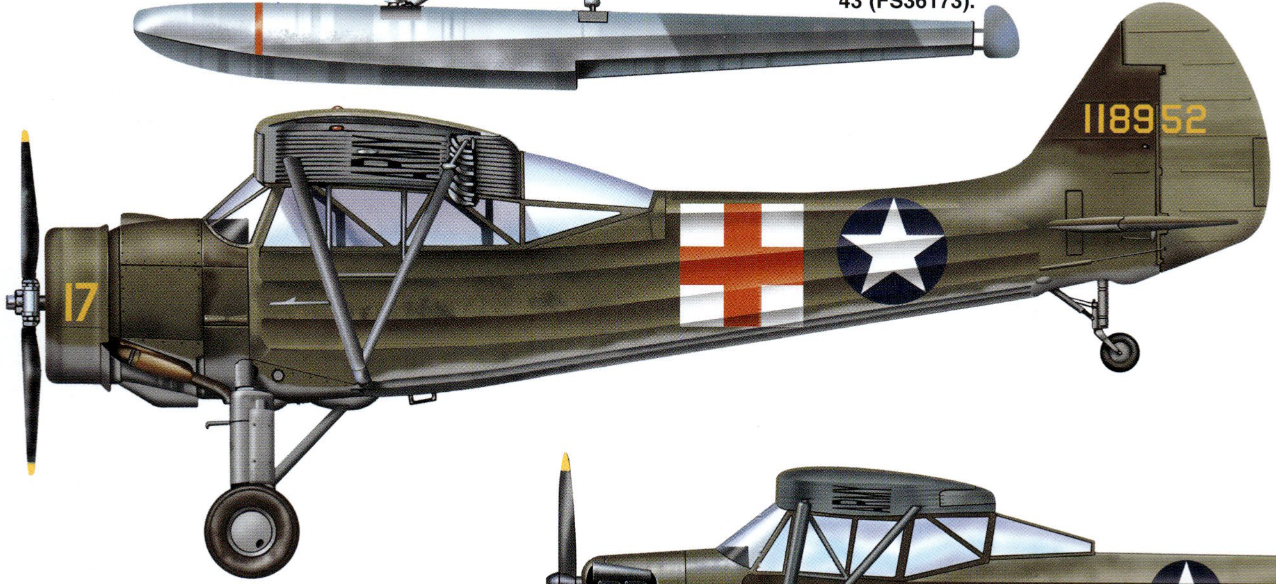

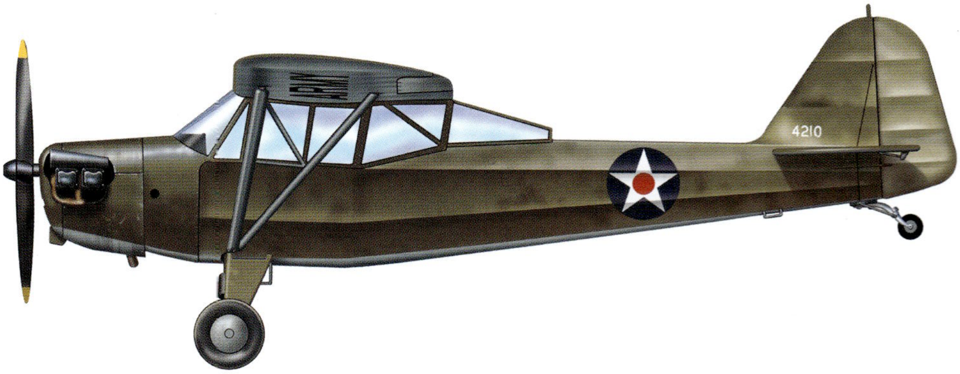

This Taylorcraft O-57 (later L-2) Grasshopper (4210) was assigned to an unknown US Army Air Forces (USAAF) liaison squadron in 1941. The national insignia was painted on the fuselage sides, upper left wing, and lower right wing. The number painted on the tail does not correspond with the serial number, which is unknown for this Grasshopper.

An unknown USAAF unit flew this Taylorcraft TG-6-TA (103/42-58800) in late 1942. The overall Aluminum Dope aircraft was used to train glider pilots destined to fly Waco CG-4 gliders for the invasion of Europe and to introduce fledgling pilots to the art of flying. The TG-6 carried a crew of three: two students and an instructor.

This Aeronca L-3 (43-2658) was an ex-O-58 assigned to the US Field Artillery (FA) until it was presented to the Free French Army in North Africa in 1943. GRASS HOPPER is camouflaged in Olive Drab over Neutral Gray, with an Orange-Yellow (ANA-614; FS33538) surround to the fuselage US national insignia. French colors are painted on the L-3's rudder.

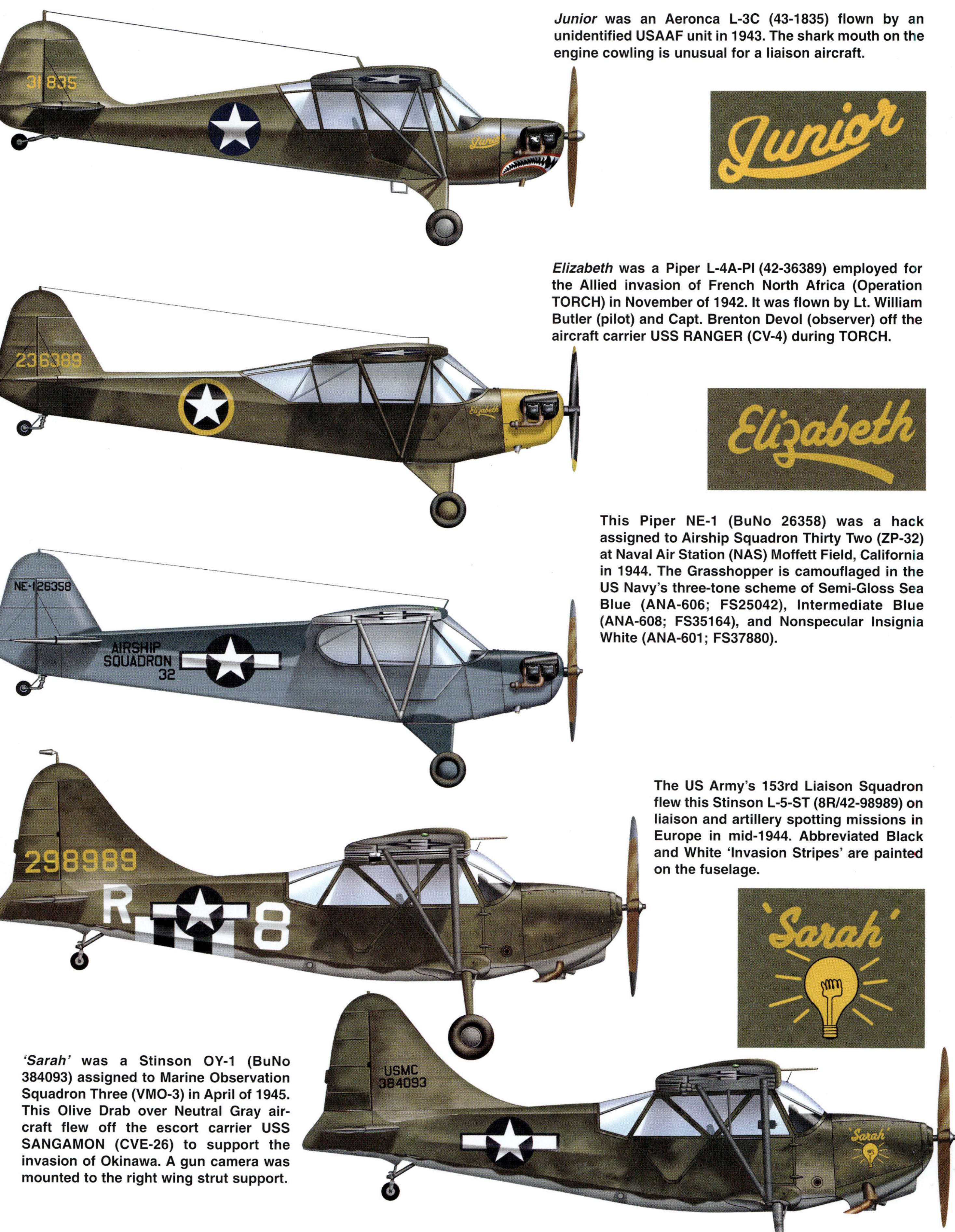

Junior was an Aeronca L-3C (43-1835) flown by an unidentified USAAF unit in 1943. The shark mouth on the engine cowling is unusual for a liaison aircraft.

Elizabeth was a Piper L-4A-PI (42-36389) employed for the Allied invasion of French North Africa (Operation TORCH) in November of 1942. It was flown by Lt. William Butler (pilot) and Capt. Brenton Devol (observer) off the aircraft carrier USS RANGER (CV-4) during TORCH.

This Piper NE-1 (BuNo 26358) was a hack assigned to Airship Squadron Thirty Two (ZP-32) at Naval Air Station (NAS) Moffett Field, California in 1944. The Grasshopper is camouflaged in the US Navy's three-tone scheme of Semi-Gloss Sea Blue (ANA-606; FS25042), Intermediate Blue (ANA-608; FS35164), and Nonspecular Insignia White (ANA-601; FS37880).

The US Army's 153rd Liaison Squadron flew this Stinson L-5-ST (8R/42-98989) on liaison and artillery spotting missions in Europe in mid-1944. Abbreviated Black and White 'Invasion Stripes' are painted on the fuselage.

'Sarah' was a Stinson OY-1 (BuNo 384093) assigned to Marine Observation Squadron Three (VMO-3) in April of 1945. This Olive Drab over Neutral Gray aircraft flew off the escort carrier USS SANGAMON (CVE-26) to support the invasion of Okinawa. A gun camera was mounted to the right wing strut support.

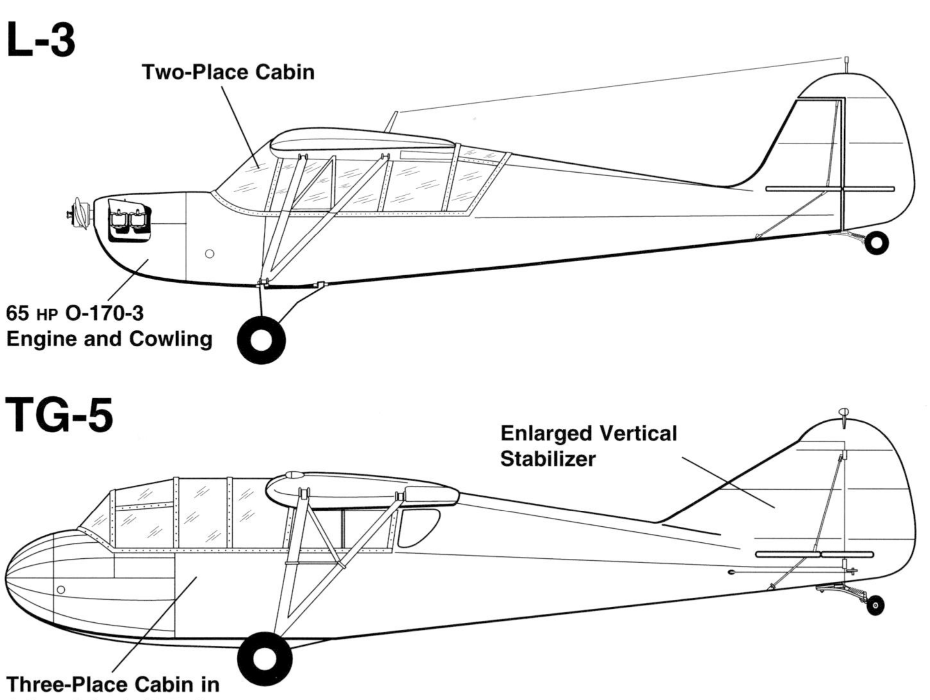

An L-3C (43-1657) rests on the grass ramp at the Lunken Airport, Cincinnati in late 1942. The aircraft's serial number was written in White chalk on the vertical stabilizer before 31657 was permanently painted in flat Orange-Yellow (ANA-614; FS33538). The observer's position had a large glass area, which provided a great view for spotting artillery or for observing enemy positions or movement. (US Army)

L-3

TG-5

Aeronca produced 253 TG-5 training gliders utilizing the L-3's fuselage, wings, and an enlarged vertical stabilizer. The three-man crew – two students and a flight instructor – sat in tandem. The TG-5's 1825-pound (828 KG) maximum gross weight was the same as for the L-3C. This overall Aluminum TG-5 (43-57358) has the Aeronca emblem painted in Black on the vertical stabilizer (National Archives)

The US Army 'bailed' (loaned) three L-3Cs to the US Navy, which designated the aircraft as JR-1s. The USAAF serial numbers and the US Navy Bureau Numbers (BuNos) for these aircraft are unknown. The JR-1s were evaluated and operated at Brown Field, Naval Auxiliary Air Station (NAS) Otay Mesa, California. The JR-1 was camouflaged with flat M-485 Blue-Gray (FS35189) upper surfaces and flat Light Gray (ANA-602; FS36440) undersurfaces. The temporary civil registration N47051 is painted on this aircraft's vertical stabilizer. (Via Terry Love)

A French Catholic priest blesses an ex-US Army L-3C (43-2658) being transferred to the Free French forces in North Africa in late 1942. The vertical stabilizer is painted in the French colors of (from front) flat French Blue (FS25090), flat White 46 (FS37875), and flat Bright Red (ANA-509; FS31136). The US national insignia retains the Orange-Yellow surround used during Operation TORCH, the Allied invasion of French North Africa. The Orange-Yellow letters FA above the tail number (2658) indicated assignment to the Field Artillery. (Via Terry Love)

The Civil Aeronautics Administration (CAA) War Training Service (WTS) used this modified L-3C (28/WTS439) in 1943. Thin wooden panels replaced the rear glass area and no radio is fitted. This L-3C is painted overall Olive Drab, with Orange-Yellow cowl, rudder, and wing tips. WTS 439 is Black on the rudder and Orange-Yellow on the left wing undersurface, while 28 is Orange-Yellow on the vertical stabilizer. The WTS received most of the 490 L-3Cs Aeronca built during 1943. (National Archives)

Piper L-4 (O-59) Grasshopper

The Piper Aircraft Company of Lock Haven, Pennsylvania was the third of three manufacturers the US Army contacted in mid-1941. Piper provided eight **J-3C-65 Cub** aircraft for US Army Air Forces (USAAF) evaluation during military exercises held that year. The J-3C-65s were delivered in civilian Yellow paint finish with a caricature of a grasshopper smoking a cigarette on the fuselage sides. Some of these Cubs were eventually painted in the then-standard camouflage scheme of Olive Drab 41 (ANA-613; FS34087) upper surfaces and Neutral Gray 43 (FS36173) undersurfaces, with a White smoking grasshopper on the fuselage. These aircraft were successfully employed during maneuvers held at Fort Bliss, Texas in July of 1941. This led the US Army to issue a contract for four Piper J-3C-65 Cubs (serial numbers 42-460/463), which were designated as **YO-59s**.

The YO-59 was a braced high-wing monoplane with a fixed landing gear. It was constructed of steel and aluminum with a wood wing spar and covered by doped fabric. The YO-59 had a wingspan of 35 feet 2 inches (10.7 M), a length of 22 feet 4 inches (6.8 M), and a height of 6 feet 8 inches (2 M). Its empty weight was 740 pounds (336 KG) and the maximum takeoff weight was 1220 pounds (553 KG).

A 65 HP Continental O-170-3 four-cylinder, air-cooled, horizontally-opposed ('flat') engine turned a two-bladed wooden fixed-pitch propeller. This powerplant gave the YO-59 a top speed of 87 MPH (140 KMH). It had a service ceiling of 11,500 feet (3505 M) and a range of 260 miles (418 KM). The two-man crew – pilot and observer – sat in tandem within the enclosed cockpit. The USAAF redesignated its Observation aircraft as Liaison aircraft in April of 1942, and the four YO-59s became **L-4s**. Four L-4s were supplied to Great Britain, which designated them **Cub Is** for evaluation.

The **O-59** was the initial production model, with Piper completing 140 aircraft (42-7813/7952). Forty O-59s were used during maneuvers held in Mississippi, Tennessee, and Texas during August and September of 1941. Each O-59 – equipped with a 6-volt electrical system and military radio equipment – cost $2230.00. The O-59 was redesignated as the L-4 in 1942.

The **O-59A** was an improved O-59 with an enlarged and widened observer's position. This allowed the rear seat to rotate 180° and face rearward. Additionally, the observer's glass area was increased to the side and above as in the Taylorcraft O-57A/L-2A. Piper built 671 O-59As (42-15159/15329 and 42-36325/36824), which were renamed L-4As in the Spring of 1942. A further 277 aircraft were delivered as **L-4A-PIs** (PI was the USAAF code for Piper) and assigned serial numbers 42-38380/38457 and 43-29048/29246.

The L-4A was the first of the light aircraft to go to war. This baptism of fire occurred during the Allied invasion of French North Africa (Operation TORCH). On 9 November 1942, three L-4As flew from the deck of the aircraft carrier USS RANGER (CV-4) to provide artillery observation for the large US naval guns. These L-4As had Orange-Yellow (ANA-614; FS33538) cowlings and an Orange-Yellow ring around the fuselage national insignias for identification. Many L-4As served in the training role in the US and were painted overall Aluminum dope (FS17178).

The 980 **L-4Bs** (43-491/1470) procured for the US Army Field Artillery was similar to the L-4A, but without radios or an electrical system. It was discovered after L-4Bs were delivered to various artillery aviation units that dust clogged carburetors while the Grasshoppers operated from unimproved airfields. This resulted in a carburetor air filter being installed in the front lower cowling, which kept dust out of the engine. Some L-4Bs were retrofitted with SCR-610 radio transmitter/receivers that operated on frequencies compatible with ground units' radios. The British Royal Air Force (RAF) used one L-4B that was serialed VM286.

The USAAF impressed 107 civilian Cubs into service. These included eight **Model J-3Ls**

A Piper J-3C-65 Cub (4/NX28202), sits in the sun at Biggs Army Air Field, Texas in 1941. The Orange-Yellow aircraft has a Black fuselage lightning stripe and a grasshopper emblem on the fuselage. The latter insignia befitted its role as an aircraft operating from grass airfields. Piper provided eight radio-equipped Cubs to the US Army for evaluation during the 1941 maneuvers. Lt. Col. Dwight D. Eisenhower – the future General and US President – borrowed one J-3C-65 for some recreational flying. He had nothing but praise for the little Cub. (US Army)

A civilian J-3C-65 pulls up to a county gasoline station for refueling during one of the many maneuvers conducted in 1941. A contingent of US Army Cavalry rides past the Grasshopper. Its upper surfaces are painted Olive Drab, with a White cross to designate the White Force and a White aircraft number (6) on the rudder. The grasshopper emblem was modified to add a hat and a smoking cigarette in the insect's mouth. (Terry Love)

The second YO-59 (42-461) is tied down near a filling station gas pump at Hawkins Field, Jackson, Mississippi on 17 September 1941. A Red cross painted on the fuselage indicates assignment to the Red Force for the maneuvers. The Grasshopper used civilian automobile fuel, which was approximately 80-octane in 1941. Eventually, 80/87-octane aviation fuel was used as the aircraft were integrated into service. The drag cone atop the rudder pulls a low frequency wire radio antenna to various lengths behind the aircraft. This tunes the radio to the proper frequency. (Boardman C. Reed)

A Piper O-59 (42-7815) sits on a compass rose at Wright Field, Dayton, Ohio. A compass rose is used to calibrate the aircraft's compass. The O-59 is camouflaged in an Olive Drab over Neutral Gray scheme that was the USAAF's standard finish from 1942 through 1945. U. S. and ARMY are painted across the wing undersurfaces in flat Black. The national insignia's Red disc was removed from all US aircraft by 1 June 1942. (US Army)

(designated **L-4Cs**), five **Model J-3Fs** (L-4Ds), 17 **Model J-4Es** (L-4Es), 43 **Model J-5As** (**L-4Fs**), and 34 **Model J-5Bs** (**L-4Gs**). Seven Cubs were impressed in Panama and employed as light cargo aircraft. The four J-5As were designated as **UC-83s**, two J-3Ls became **UC-83As**, and one J-4A was renamed the **UC-83B**. The British also impressed a number of civilian Cubs for use as trainers and unit hacks.

The **L-4H** was an improved version of the L-4B. The L-4H was not fitted with an electrical system or radio equipment, but did receive an upgraded hydraulic braking system. A one-piece windshield replaced the three-piece windshield installed on earlier variants. Piper completed 1801 L-4Hs (43-29247/30547 and 44-79545/80044) – the most widely produced variant of the early liaison aircraft.

The **L-4J** was the last wartime J-65 Cub production model, with 1680 aircraft built (44-80045/80844, 45-4401/5200, and 45-55175/55254). This variant was nearly identical to the L-4H, but some L-4Js replaced the fixed-pitch propeller with a Beech-Roby controllable pitch propeller. This was intended to improve take off performance. The Beech-Roby propellers were not successful and were soon replaced with a fixed-pitch type. Piper built 5553 L-4s for the USAAF during World War Two.

The US Navy also procured J-3C-65s directly from Piper and designated them as **NE-1s**; N designated Trainer and E was the Navy's designator for Piper Aircraft. The Navy acquired 230 NE-1s and they were assigned Bureau Numbers (BuNos) of 226196 through 226425. The NE-1 featured dual controls and was painted either overall Orange-Yellow or Aluminum. Twenty additional aircraft (BuNos 29669/29688) were later ordered and were designated **NE-2**. These aircraft were similar to the Army's L-4J and were equipped with controllable pitch propellers.

The **HE-1** was the US Navy's designation for 100 modified Piper J-5C Cub Cruisers acquired in 1942. These aircraft had a modified turtle deck that was hinged upward at the front. This allowed a litter to be placed in the modified rear fuselage. H stood for Ambulance, but the US Navy changed this to A in 1943, when helicopters began to enter service. This resulted in the HE-1 becoming the **AE-1**. A 100 HP Lycoming O-235-2 four-cylinder, air-cooled, horizontally-opposed engine powered the HE-1/AE-1. Some aircraft were painted overall Aluminum and others were Orange-Yellow. AE-1s served as airfield ambulances, which were able to land close to an aircraft landing accident and bring the injured to the hospital much quicker than a ground based ambulance. Helicopters soon replaced fixed wing aircraft in that role.

Piper – as Taylorcraft did with the L-2 and Aeronca with the L-3 – also produced a training glider version of their light observation aircraft. This J-3C glider derivative was designated the **TG-8**. The Cub's engine and fuel system were removed and a new nose section complete with flight controls was bolted directly to the former motor mounts. This 8-inch (20.3 CM) longer nose increased the glider's length to 23 feet (7 M). A hinged canopy provided entry to the front cockpit. Spoilers added to the upper wing surfaces increased landing angles. A modified cross-bar landing gear replaced the J-3C's Vee-type gear. The USAAF's Training Command ordered 250 TG-8s (43-3009/3258), with the US Navy ordering three additional aircraft designated **XLNT-1s**. The latter were originally assigned USAAF serials 43-12496/12498 before they were delivered with the BuNos 36428/36430.

Some L-4s flew off US Navy Landing Ships, Tank (LSTs) beginning with the Allied invasion of Sicily (Operation HUSKY) on 10 July 1943. A Pierced Steel Planking (PSP) 'flight deck' was built to allow the L-4 to take off. The Grasshopper's pilot was fully aware that he could not land back on the ship, due to its lack of aircraft recovery equipment. Only two LSTs received this improvised flight deck.

A few L-4s were modified with nose-mounted steel hooks. These Grasshoppers were assigned to LSTs equipped with the Brodie Device, which was developed by Captain Jeff Brodie. This device was a 300-foot (91.4 M) long cable strung between two towers. A hook-equipped L-4 could either land or take off from this cable. The tower and cables were first tested on the ground and were then fitted to several LSTs. The Brodie Device was first used dur-

The third production O-59 (42-7815) was essentially a civilian J-3C-65 Cub equipped with a military radio. The Grasshopper was evaluated at Wright Field and was camouflaged in Olive Drab over Neutral Gray, with the national insignia in four positions (both fuselage sides, upper left wing, and lower right wing). (US Army)

ing the US invasion of Okinawa (Operation ICEBERG) on 1 April 1945.

L-4s carried no armament apart from the crew's personal weapons, but many Grasshoppers were 'field armed' with 2.36-inch (60MM) M1/M9 'Bazooka' rocket launchers fitted to the wing struts. Some L-4 were also fitted with bomb shackles and armed with hand grenades. One L-4 was actually credited with destroying a few German tanks.

The L-4 played an important role during World War Two, providing everything from pilot training to artillery spotting, ambulance duties, to – in a few cases – attack aircraft. When the little yellow civilian Piper Cub went to war as the L-4 Grasshopper, it would soon be bestowed the nickname 'Maytag Messerschmitt.' (This referred to the US appliance manufacturer Maytag and the German Messerschmitt Bf 109 fighter.) The L-4 went on to serve in the Korean War (1950-1953) until the Cessna L-19 (later O-1) Bird Dog replaced the Grasshopper during the early 1950s.

The L-4 (ex O-59) lacked an electric engine starter and it was necessary to manually start the engine by spinning the propeller. This observer starts his Grasshopper's engine at a mist-shrouded US airfield in southern Italy in 1943. US national insignias are the only markings painted on this aircraft, which was used to spot artillery and observe enemy movements. A Beech C-45 Expeditor transport is in the background. (Via Terry Love)

An L-4 from the II Corps Air Operations School flies over two 105MM howitzers during training in southern England on 12 March 1943. The howitzers were assigned to the 29th Infantry Division, which assaulted Omaha Beach in Normandy, France on 6 June 1944 (D-Day). The L-4's small size and low and slow flying ability made it an excellent platform for artillery observation and spotting. Piper completed 5553 L-4s during World War Two, which made this aircraft the most produced of the wartime 'L-Birds.' (US Army)

Deck crewmen position an L-4A (42-36389) named *Elizabeth* on an aircraft elevator aboard the aircraft carrier USS RANGER (CV-4) in November of 1942. This was during Operation TORCH, the Allied invasion of French North Africa. Both the cowling and the fuselage national insignia surround are Orange-Yellow. Most of these crew wear M1 steel 'pot' helmets and carry gas masks. The L-4A's left wing shows some signs of repair and overpainting with mismatched paint. (National Archives)

The US Army ordered 250 TG-8 unpowered training gliders, which were modified from L-4Bs. The modifications included removing the Lycoming O-170 engine, fuel tank, and rubber sprung landing gear. An extended greenhouse for the three-man crew and a steel sprung single axle landing gear were installed. This TG-8 is painted in an overall Aluminum dope over the fabric covering. (National Archives)

A row of L-4A trainers sits on a grass ramp at Fort Sill, Oklahoma in 1943. The L-4 was used as an introductory trainer to determine the student aviator's primary skills. These Grasshoppers are in overall Aluminum (FS17178) doped canvas, while the propellers and spinners are painted flat Black. The Black paint was later discovered to actually hold in moisture, which caused the laminated wooden propellers to disintegrate. By 1945, all L-4 propellers were left in a natural finish. (US Army)

L-4

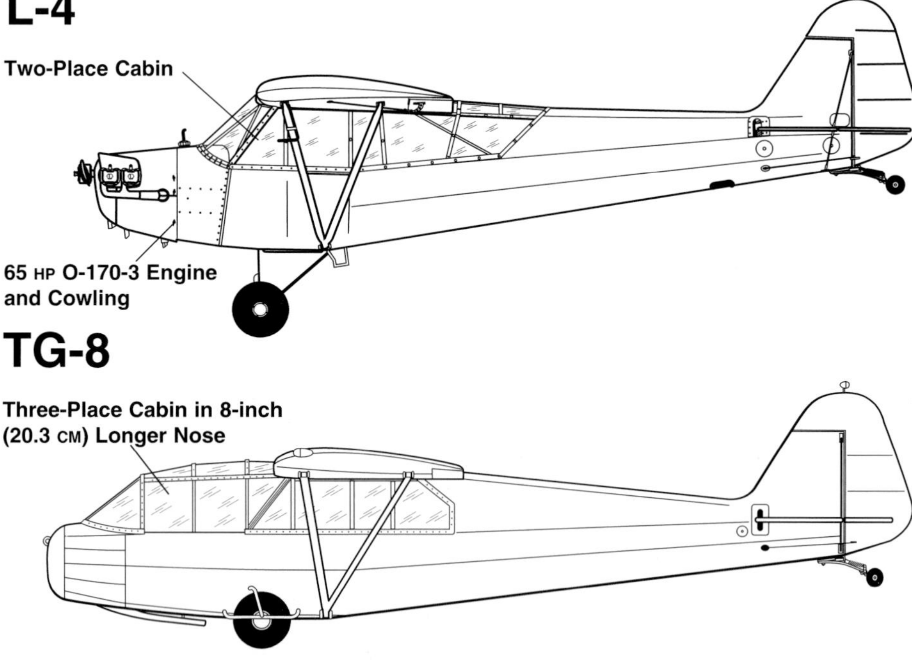

TG-8

A Fifth Army L-4B (43-1105) is positioned on the temporary flight deck on USS LST-386, a US Navy Landing Ship, Tank (LST). This occurred during Operation HUSKY, the Allied invasion of Sicily on 10 July 1943. The tail wheel is placed in an elevated box as the L-4 sits on a flight deck made from Perforated Steel Planking (PSP). An Orange-Yellow ring is painted around the fuselage national insignia. The Orange-Yellow letter FA above the tail number 31105 indicated the L-4's assignment to the Field Artillery (FA). (US Army)

A temporary flight deck was fitted to LST-525 to accommodate L-4s from the 131st and 460th Parachute Field Artillery Battalions, Fifth Army. These units participated in the Allied invasion of Southern France (Operation ANVIL) on 15 August 1944. L-4s were placed on outriggers and brought up for flight once the deck was cleared. Rudders were removed from these Grasshoppers to allow flight deck clearance for aircraft taking off. (US Army)

Two mechanics tend to an L-4 named 'PAPPY' as it sits under a Boeing B-17G Flying Fortress bomber somewhere in England. The mechanic to the left gestures with his leather mallet while making a point to his colleague seated on the right landing gear tire. An air driven electrical generator for the radio is mounted between the main landing gear struts. The cowling's forward section is painted Bright Red (ANA-509; FS31136). Many L-4s flew across the English Channel on and following the 6 June 1944 Allied invasion of France (Operation OVERLORD). (Via Squadron/Signal Publications)

A 153rd Liaison Squadron (LS) L-4 is prepared for flight from an airbase in England, which is believed to be Membury. The observer already occupies the rear seat and the engine is ticking over as the pilot prepares for flight. The cowling's nose appears to be Orange-Yellow and the propeller spinner appears to be flat Bright Red. The 153rd LS performed photoreconnaissance and spotting duties while stationed in England.

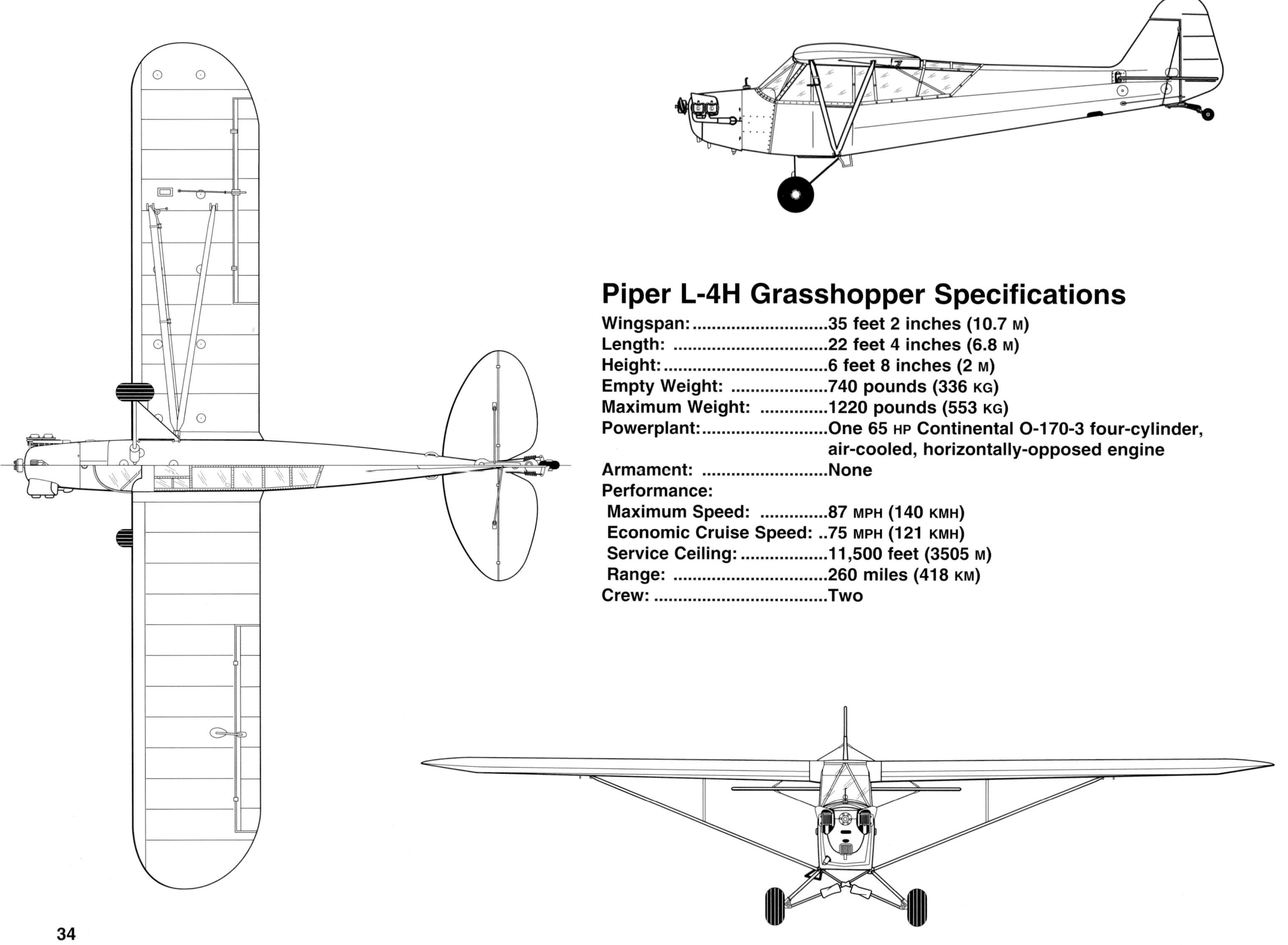

Piper L-4H Grasshopper Specifications
Wingspan: 35 feet 2 inches (10.7 M)
Length: 22 feet 4 inches (6.8 M)
Height: 6 feet 8 inches (2 M)
Empty Weight: 740 pounds (336 KG)
Maximum Weight: 1220 pounds (553 KG)
Powerplant: One 65 HP Continental O-170-3 four-cylinder, air-cooled, horizontally-opposed engine
Armament: None
Performance:
Maximum Speed: 87 MPH (140 KMH)
Economic Cruise Speed: 75 MPH (121 KMH)
Service Ceiling: 11,500 feet (3505 M)
Range: 260 miles (418 KM)
Crew: Two

A friendly dog looks on as a pilot begins to start the engine of an L-4J (24-<u>A</u>/45-4500) named "LUCKY FORWARD." Both Artillery Headquarters and Third Army Commander Lt. General George S. Patton, Jr. used this L-4J, the latter as his personal aircraft. A Stinson L-5 (53-<u>A</u>) from the 4th Armored Division sits on the PSP ramp in the background. (US Army)

An L-4A kicks up some dust while taking off from a volcanic rock road in Hawaii in 1943. The pilot's right rudder and aileron position corrects for a crosswind. The cowling was painted either Orange-Yellow or Insignia White for identification. The L-4 would 'unstick' (become airborne) at approximately 35 knots (40 мрн/64 кмн) and land at approximately the same speed with a moderate headwind. It was said that anybody that could land a Piper Cub could land anything, as the aircraft tended to 'float' (hang in the air) due to the lack of wing flaps. (US Army)

An Enlisted Sergeant Pilot (E-6 Grade) stands by an L-4J (56-J/44-80570) assigned to the 7th Armored Division, 12th Army Group. The Grasshopper is tied down in a field while undergoing maintenance in 1945. The propeller is left in natural wood, with Bright Red tips and a spinner that appears to be either Insignia White or Orange-Yellow. The cowling is removed for easy access to the Lycoming O-170 four-cylinder engine. (Ken Danielson via Squadron/Signal Publications)

An L-4H (426/43-29280) hangs off a cable attached to the Brodie Device during a test of this apparatus. The Brodie Device was designed to launch and recover aircraft on cables strung between two towers on a US Navy LST. The device mounted to the cowl and fuselage was designed to catch a cable when landing or launching. (US Army)

An L-4 hangs from the Brodie Device cable just off the port bow of USS LST-776 during Pacific Ocean operations in 1945. Another Grasshopper is spotted on the ship's foredeck near the Brodie Device tower, while a third L-4 is mounted on an amidships catapult angled to starboard. (Real War Photos)

This L-4 – equipped with a Brodie Device hook – made a hard landing, which damaged the main undercarriage. The Grasshopper is painted in overall Aluminum dope, as are the other undamaged L-4 trainers sharing the field. The rope on the ground was used to lift the L-4 onto a trailer that took the aircraft to a hangar for landing gear repairs. (US Army)

The Brodie Device-equipped LST-776 steams in the Pacific in 1945. A cable was strung from fore and aft towers angled just off the port side. A crane raised an L-4 or Stinson L-5 from the LST's deck to the cable. The pilot then entered the aircraft while it hung from the cable. Faint-hearted pilots need not apply, because a slip meant they were in the water. (Via Terry Love)

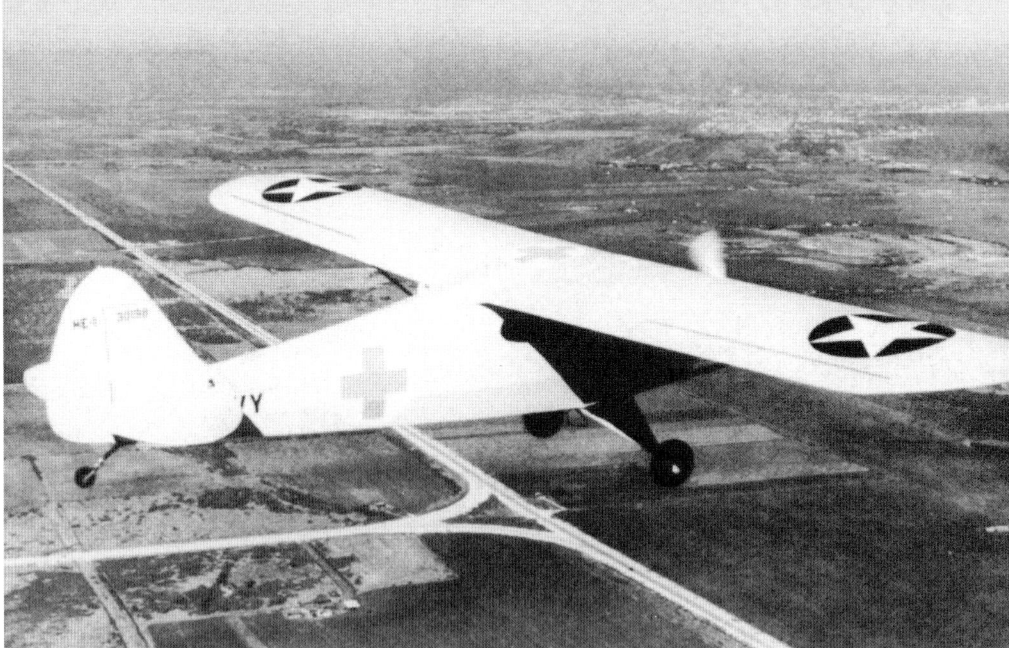

The US Navy designated the J-5C Cub Cruiser as the HE-1. H stood for Hospital (i.e., Ambulance) and E was the US Navy's code for Piper. This HE-1 (BuNo 30275) was one of 100 aircraft modified into flying ambulances, which were each powered by a 100 HP Lycoming O-235-2 four-cylinder engine. The aft fuselage was hinged just behind the wing root and opened upward to accept a litter. The US Navy painted the HE-1 in either overall Aluminum or Orange-Yellow with Black lettering. (National Archives)

A 2nd Marine Air Wing (MAW) Curtiss R5C-1 Commando (34) unloads an AE-1 somewhere in the Pacific. The AE-1 is finished in overall Aluminum dope, with Bright Red crosses replacing the US national insignia. A Bright Red diagonal stripe was painted on the vertical tail. AE-1s flew wounded aircrew from crash sites to hospitals near their home airfields. (Via Terry Love)

An HE-1 (BuNo 30198) flies from Naval Air Station (NAS) Corpus Christi, Texas in 1942. This aircraft is believed to be in overall Aluminum with Black aft fuselage and tail markings. Red crosses on White circles are painted on the fuselage sides and on the upper wing. In 1943, the US Navy reassigned the designation letter H to helicopters and HE-1s were redesignated AE-1s. (National Archives)

The Navy acquired 230 NE-1s, which were L-4s equipped with dual controls for training. Many NE-1s were passed to the Marines for observation and liaison duties. This NE-1 assigned to the 1st Provisional Observation Group is parked on Pavuvu in the Russell Islands in August of 1944. The Grasshopper retains its USAAF serial number (43-30170) on the vertical stabilizer. The NE-1 has Semi-Gloss Sea Blue (ANA-606; FS24042) upper surfaces and flat Neutral Gray 43 (FS36173) undersurfaces. (USMC)

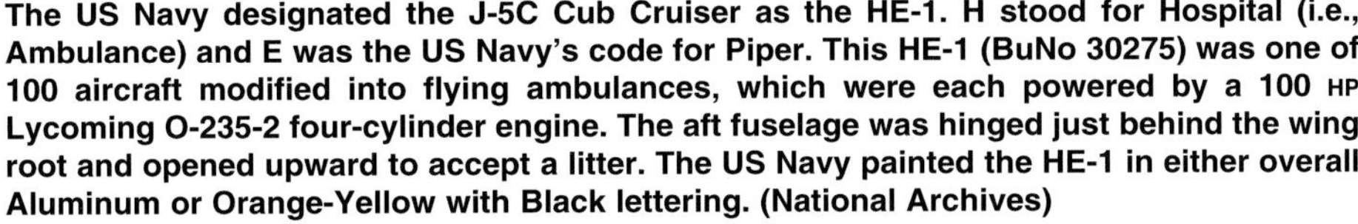

A US Army aviator prepares to enter his L-4 somewhere in Italy in 1943. A grasshopper with top hat is painted on the right fuselage side just aft of the cockpit. The pilot wears a standard issue B-3 wool-lined leather flying jacket and carries a map board and binoculars. He is about to install a battery powered SCR-610 radio in the L-4. (US Army via Terry Love)

The wings were removed and stowed alongside this L-4's fuselage at Pearl Harbor, Hawaii in 1945. The Grasshopper is loaded onto a 2 1/2-ton truck for transport to a waiting landing craft. The drogue antenna for the L-4's radio is mounted atop the rudder. This antenna pulled the wire out from the aircraft, which adjusted to the radio's proper frequency. (National Archives)

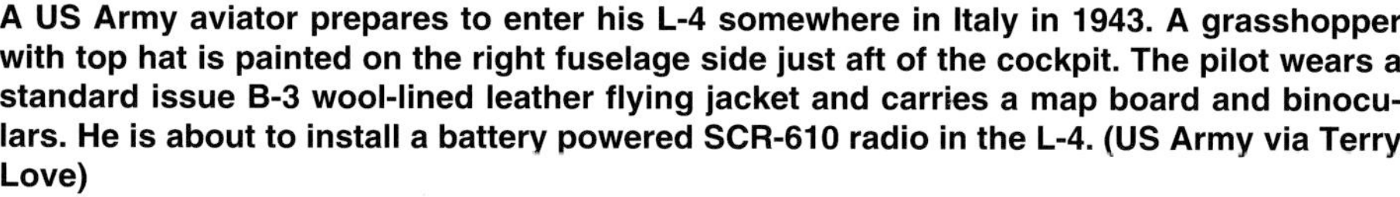

General Henry H. 'Hap' Arnold, USAAF Commanding General, sits in an L-4's rear seat during a visit to Italy in December of 1943. This Grasshopper was assigned to the US Fifth Army Headquarters, whose liaison aircraft displayed a large White A on the fuselage. Arnold's rank placard – four White stars on a Red background – is placed in the rear window. The national insignia displays the short-lived Insignia Red border authorized between June and August of 1943. (USAF)

Tailfin Drogue Antenna

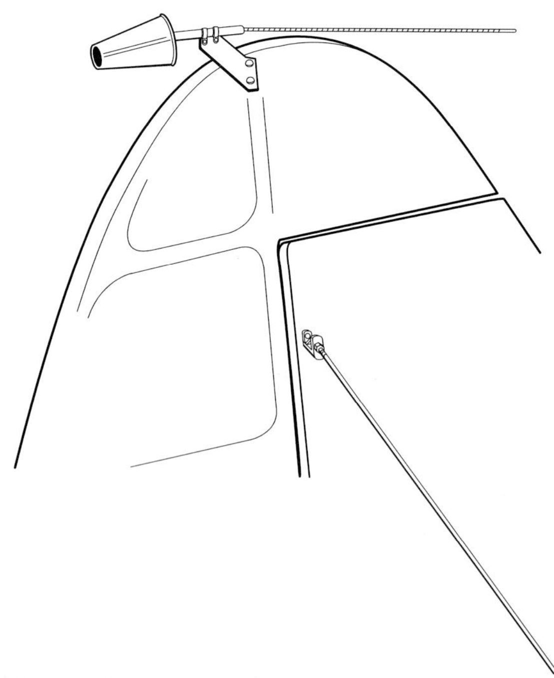

An L-4 named THUNDERBOLT (AC) prepares to take off from a grass airfield in Europe in 1944. This Grasshopper was assigned to the 68th Armored Field Artillery Battalion. A K-24 aerial camera is mounted in the open cabin door. THUNDERBOLT on the nose is believed to be painted Insignia White. L-4s flew aerial observation and liaison missions from unimproved airfields throughout World War Two in Europe. (US Army)

An L-4H pilot stands beside his Grasshopper (39-F/44-79676) on a forward airfield in France in the Summer of 1944. This variant featured a one-piece windshield that replaced the three-piece windshields of earlier L-4s. Black and White 'Invasion' stripes were painted on the wings and fuselages of Allied aircraft that supported Operation OVERLORD. (USAF)

A US soldier examines an L-4H (49-L/43-30013) parked in a hastily prepared revetment at Puffendorf, near Baesweiler, Germany on 11 December 1944. Sloped earthen berms reduced the risk of damage in the event of an air attack. This Grasshopper was assigned to the 2nd Armored Field Artillery Battalion, 2nd Armored Division. Unusually, the fuselage 'Invasion' stripes were retained on this L-4H, although the wing stripes were overpainted. These markings were usually removed weeks after the D-Day landing in France to improve the aircraft's camouflage. Two fuel cans are placed ahead of the aircraft. (National Archives)

A ground crewman brushes snow off the right wing of an L-4 (BC) parked near La Bourgance, France on 12 November 1944. The aircraft is secured to the ground using ropes tied to the wings and staked to the earth. Another Grasshopper is parked in the background. The fuselage code indicates assignment to the 10th Field Artillery Battalion, 3rd Infantry Division. (National Archives)

Several L-4s are parked on a stretch of the *Autobahn* (German superhighway) near Limburg, Germany on 27 March 1945. The right lane served as a runway, while the left lane provided ramps for the Grasshoppers. The near L-4 displays the fuselage code (67) of the 9th Armored Division, First Army. (National Archives)

Skis replaced wheels on the landing gear of this 30th Infantry Division L-4H (44-J/44-80091) near Spa, Belgium on 11 January 1945. These metal skis allowed the Grasshopper to operate from snow-covered airfields. This feature came in handy when L-4s supported US forces during the Battle of the Bulge in the winter of 1944-45. A ground crewman prepares to spin the propeller while the pilot switches on the ignition. (National Archives)

A US Army pilot prepares to start the engine of an L-4 on a dusty South Korean road. A few Grasshoppers served during the Korean War in the artillery spotting, liaison, and troop observation roles. This aircraft's cowling is believed to be painted Orange-Yellow. The Cessna L-19 (later O-1) Bird Dog eventually replaced the L-4 in US Army service during the early 1950s. (Via Terry Love)

Stinson L-5 (O-62) Sentinel

In 1941, the USAAF issued a contract to the Vultee-Stinson Aircraft Company of Wayne, Michigan. This contract called for 275 **O-62s**, a military version of the Stinson **Model 105 Voyager**. The Army's version had an increased width fuselage and military radios. Vultee had purchased Stinson Aircraft in mid-1940 so they could build Vultee aircraft – including the A-31 and A-35 Vengeance dive-bombers and the O-49/L-1 Vigilant – using Stinson's production facilities.

The **O-62-ST** (ST being the USAAF's code for Stinson) was a braced high-wing monoplane with fixed landing gear. It had wooden wing spars and ribs and welded steel tubing for the fuselage structure. The aircraft employed a doped fabric skin. The O-62 had a wingspan of 34 feet (10.4 M), an overall length of 24 feet 1 inch (7.3 M), and a height of 7 feet 1 inch (2.2 M). All subsequent O-62/L-5s had the same dimensions. Its empty weight was 1472 pounds (668 KG) and the maximum takeoff weight was 2158 pounds (979 KG). A 185 HP Lycoming O-435-1 six-cylinder, air-cooled, horizontally-opposed engine turned a two-bladed wooden fixed pitch propeller.

The O-62 had a maximum speed of 129 MPH (208 KMH) and an economical cruise speed of 100 MPH (161 KMH). Wing leading edge slots and slotted trailing edge flaps allowed the Sentinel to land at 45 MPH (72 KMH). Its service ceiling was 15,800 feet (4816 M) and its range was 450 miles (724 km). The two-man crew of pilot and observer sat in tandem within the fully enclosed cockpit.

The 275 O-62s (42-14798/15072) delivered from late 1941 were redesignated **L-5s** in April of 1942. Vultee also produced 1731 **L-5-VW** (V for Vultee; W for Wayne, Michigan) aircraft (42-14798/15702 and 42-98036/99573).

Vultee converted 688 L-5s to **L-5A** standard in 1943. A 24-volt electrical system replaced the earlier 12-volt system. This allowed for installing upgraded radios, which enabled L-5As to communicate with attack aircraft. No serial numbers were singled out and the designator was noted on the aircraft's data plate.

The **L-5B** featured a modified fuselage capable of holding 200 pounds (91 KG) of cargo or a patient on a litter. The litter was loaded through an upward hinged long door on the right upper fuselage side. The fuselage was deepened and the observer's windows were changed. Vultee completed 730 L-5Bs (42-99574/99753 and 44-16703/17252) from 1943. A few L-5Bs were fitted with upper nose hooks for operating off Brodie Device-equipped US Navy LSTs. Twin floats sometimes replaced the L-5B's landing gear for waterborne operation. The float equipped L-5B had a ventral fin added under the rear fuselage. This fin increased stability and compensated for aerodynamic changes caused by the float installation.

The 200 **L-5Cs** (44-17253/17452) were identical to L-5s, but were fitted with provisions and electrical equipment for a K-20 aerial camera. The K-20 was installed within lower fuselage brackets and operated by either the pilot or observer.

The USAAF cancelled the **L-5D** before any aircraft were built and did not assign any serial numbers. It is believed that this variant would be equipped with Handley-Page leading edge slats as on the Stinson O-49/L-1. These slats would have further improved the Sentinel's low speed performance.

The **L-5E** was similar to the L-5C, but with drooping ailerons that lowered with the flaps. These modified control surfaces improved the aircraft's low speed performance. Additionally, a stirrup step added to the lower fuselage aided entry to the observer's rear seat position. Vultee built 750 L-5Es (44-17453/18202) from late 1943.

An L-5B (44-17103) was reconfigured during production into the **XL-5F**. A 185 HP Lycoming O-435-2 six-cylinder, air-cooled, horizontally-opposed engine replaced the O-435-1 of the same horsepower. The XL-5F was converted back to L-5B standards following the engine tests.

The first production L-5 Sentinel (42-14798) sits on the ramp at Stinson's Wayne, Michigan plant in 1942. The L-5 was basically a Stinson Model V-76 Voyager with a widened fuselage and added radio equipment with its associated electrical generator. This Sentinel was camouflaged with Olive Drab upper surfaces and Neutral Gray undersurfaces. The drogue atop the rudder streamed out the radio antenna to tune the set. (US Army)

The fourth production L-5 (3/42-14801) is parked on a grass ramp in 1944. The two-bladed propeller is finished in natural wood, as opposed to the earlier Black painted types. All L-5s had fabric covering a welded steel and wood construction. A 185 HP Lycoming O-435-1 six-cylinder, air-cooled, horizontally-opposed ('flat') engine gave the Sentinel a maximum speed of 129 MPH (208 KMH). (US Army)

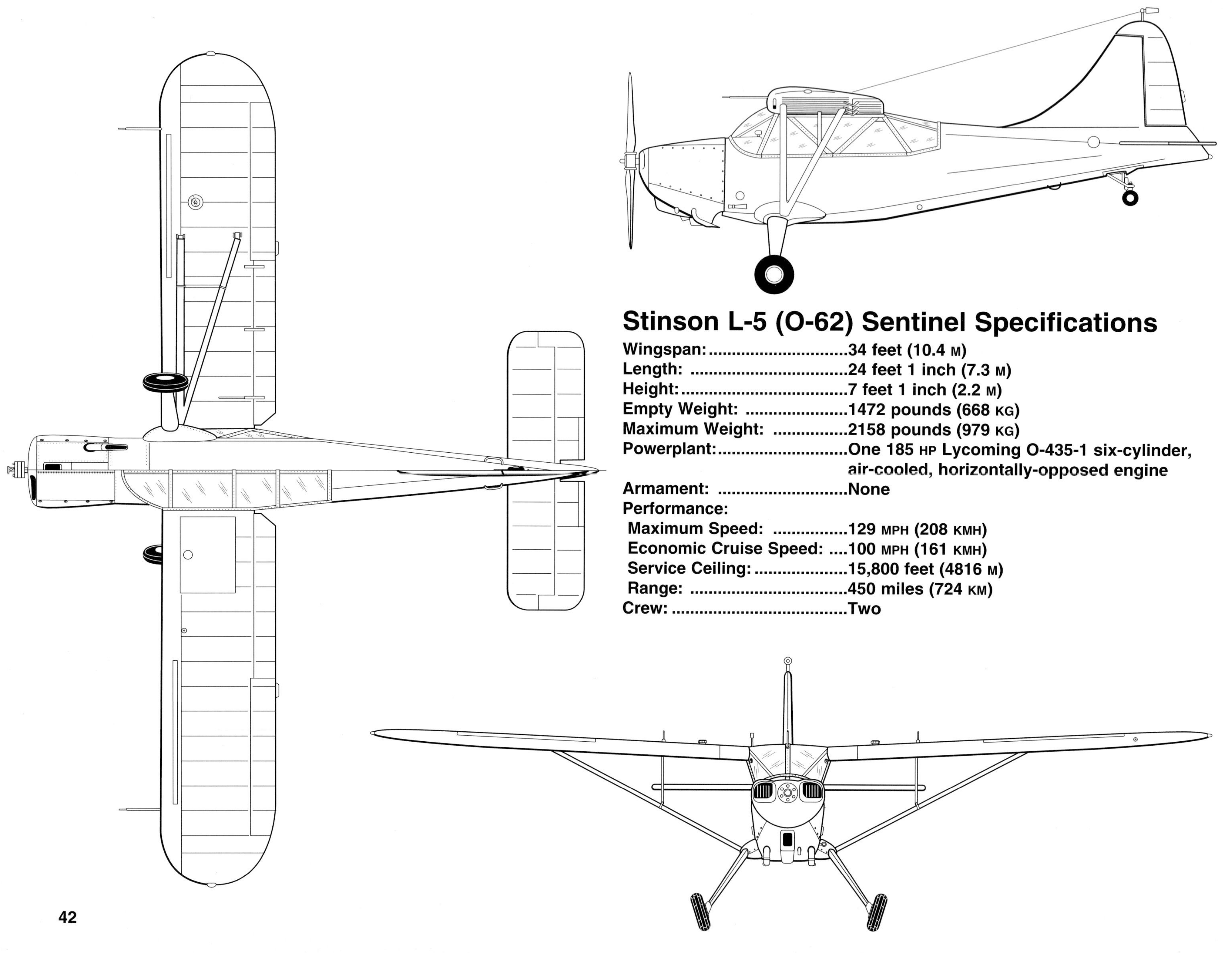

Stinson L-5 (O-62) Sentinel Specifications
Wingspan:..............................34 feet (10.4 M)
Length: ....24 feet 1 inch (7.3 M)
Height:...................................7 feet 1 inch (2.2 M)
Empty Weight: ....1472 pounds (668 KG)
Maximum Weight: ....2158 pounds (979 KG)
Powerplant:............................One 185 HP Lycoming O-435-1 six-cylinder,
air-cooled, horizontally-opposed engine
Armament: ....None
Performance:
Maximum Speed: ....129 MPH (208 KMH)
Economic Cruise Speed: ....100 MPH (161 KMH)
Service Ceiling: ....15,800 feet (4816 M)
Range: ....450 miles (724 KM)
Crew: ....Two

A ground crewman prepares to load a 25th Liaison Squadron (LS) L-5 (42-98712) on an airfield in New Guinea in 1944. The 25th LS was named the 'Guinea Short Lines' since they operated not only in the liaison role, but also on transport, ambulance, and search and rescue missions. GUINEA SHORT LINES is painted in White above a White kangaroo on the Sentinel's cowling. The 25th LS later deployed to the Philippines in support of US operations there in 1944-45. (Via Terry Love)

The last Sentinel production variant was the **L-5G**, which was an L-5E with a 190 HP Lycoming O-435-11 six-cylinder, air-cooled, horizontally-opposed engine. The L-5G featured enlarged wheels and tires, plus an improved braking system for superior rough field performance. An improved SCR-274N radio was installed for communicating with ground forces and other aircraft. The slightly increased horsepower gave the L-5G a maximum speed of 130 MPH (209 KMH), despite a gross weight that increased to 2200 pounds (998 KG). Vultee built 115 L-5Gs (45-34911/35025) late in World War Two. This brought total Sentinel production during World War Two to 3801 aircraft. One additional L-5G (57-6278) was completed as a glider tug for the US Air Force Academy in Colorado Springs, Colorado in 1957.

The USAAF also impressed civilian Voyagers into wartime service. These included eight **Model 10 Voyagers (L-9As)** and 12 **Model 10A Voyagers (L-9Bs)**.

L-5s saw extensive liaison and observation service with US Army units in Europe, the Pacific, and the China-Burma-India (CBI) Theater of Operations. The Sentinel's 15,800-foot service ceiling was appreciated in the CBI, where the 1st Air Commando Group and other units flew missions near the Himalayan Mountain range. The US supplied 100 L-5s to the British, who designated them **Sentinel I** and **IIs**. Royal Air Force units flew Sentinels in the CBI Theater.

The USAAF transferred 306 L-5s of several variants to the US Navy during World War Two. The Navy assigned these aircraft to the US Marine Corps under the designation **OY**. (O stood for Observation, while Y designated Consolidated, which acquired Vultee in 1943.) Most Sentinels were standard configuration **OY-1s**, but at least 29 aircraft were modified with ambulance equipment and designated as **OY-2s**. The Marines flew OYs in the Pacific Theater.

The US Army, Air Force, and Marines deployed L-5s to Korea in 1950. They flew Forward Air Control (FAC) missions alongside North American T-6 Texans that were nicknamed 'Mosquitoes.' Surviving L-5-VWs and L-5G-VWs were redesignated as **U-19A-VWs** and

The Lycoming O-435-1 engine of this II Corps Artillery L-5 (B/42-98947) undergoes maintenance at Piccioli, Italy in 1944. All of the engine cylinders ('jugs'), rods, and pistons were removed in order to rebuild the engine. Light aircraft mechanics had to operate in the most severe of conditions in order to keep the aircraft operational. (US Army)

A float-equipped L-5 (S-5/42-15025) takes off from Lake Lawtonka, near Fort Sill, Oklahoma in 1944. It was undergoing tests to determine the floatplane's suitability for field use. Water rudders fitted to the aft ends of the EDO floats aided in controlling the aircraft on the water. An auxiliary ventral fin added to the aft fuselage of float-equipped L-5s aided in-flight stability. (US Army)

U-19B-VWs, respectively, in September of 1962. The new designations conformed with the unified US Department of Defense military designator system. The last U-19s were retired from US military service by the mid-1960s.

Medium Green 42 (ANA-612; FS34092) scallops are painted on the Olive Drab upper wing and tail surfaces of this L-5 (42-99461) in 1944. A photographic calibration disc appears on the engine cowling. The Sentinel's rudder was replaced, but the Orange-Yellow serial number was not fully repainted on the aircraft. Various fuselage fabric areas show signs of repaired damage and repainting, which resulted in darker colored areas on the aft fuselage. (Via Terry Love)

An L-5 (104/42-98316) flies over a mountain range somewhere in the CBI Theater of Operations. The Sentinel's 15,800-foot (4816 M) service ceiling was useful for operating in mountainous areas that were common in this Theater. This aircraft's cowling appears to be painted in Red. The aft fuselage and tail show signs of repainting. The national insignia on the fuselage is believed to have a Red outline. (US Army)

An L-5 (32-K/42-98242) assigned to the 119th Field Artillery Group Headquarters, Fifth Army is parked on a grassy ramp in France in mid-1944. The code is painted as K-32 on the cowling. Two other Sentinels rest in the background. Wrap-around Black and White 'Invasion' stripes are painted on the fuselage and outer wings. This L-5 was utilized during the Allied invasion of France (Operation OVERLORD) on 6 June 1944. (Via Terry Love)

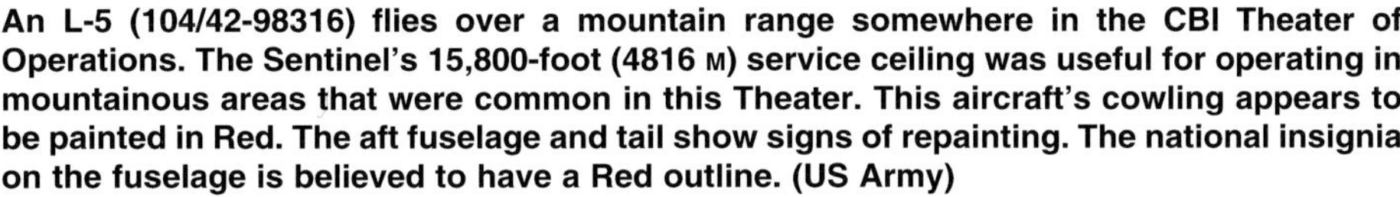

This L-5 (42-14891) was employed on armament feasibility tests in the US in October of 1944. Two rocket tubes – one per wing – were mounted on the wing struts, along with electrical firing mechanisms. Rockets would have been used to mark targets and possibly attack soft targets. (Via Terry Love)

A 2.36-inch (60MM) rocket tube was fitted to the left wing strut of this 5th LS L-5 (42-99273) deployed to the China-Burma-India (CBI) Theater of Operations. The US Army tested the feasibility of rocket armament on L-5s in the US, but never authorized their operational use. US troops added rocket launchers as field modifications to Sentinels. An Insignia White band is painted across the vertical tail's upper section. (Via Terry Love)

This 5th LS L-5B OKLAHOMA HAWK (44-16829) flies over Burma in 1944. An Insignia White horizontal stripe painted across the vertical tail was a Squadron recognition marking. The L-5B was basically an L-5A with a deeper rear fuselage and provisions for either a stretcher or 200 pounds (91 KG) of cargo. (US Army)

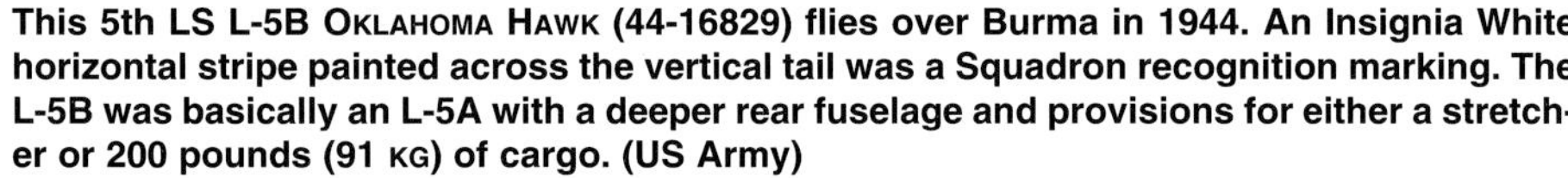

Both the pilot's window and the ambulance door are folded down on this L-5C (44-17273). A 150-gallon (568 L) aluminum drop tank strapped to the observer/cargo area was used either to transport fuel to another airfield or to supplement the Sentinel's internal fuel. The L-5C was basically an L-5B, but with provisions for a K-20 aerial camera on the right wing strut rack. (Via Terry Love)

An aerial observer slides down the Brodie Device entry cable to enter an already running L-5B (82/44-16835) aerial ambulance. The Sentinel's flaps are lowered and the aircraft soon sped down the cable to take off. You did not have to be a trapeze artist to operate from the Brodie Device, but it would have helped. Pilots and observers with a fear of heights need not apply. (US Army)

L-5 (Left Profile)

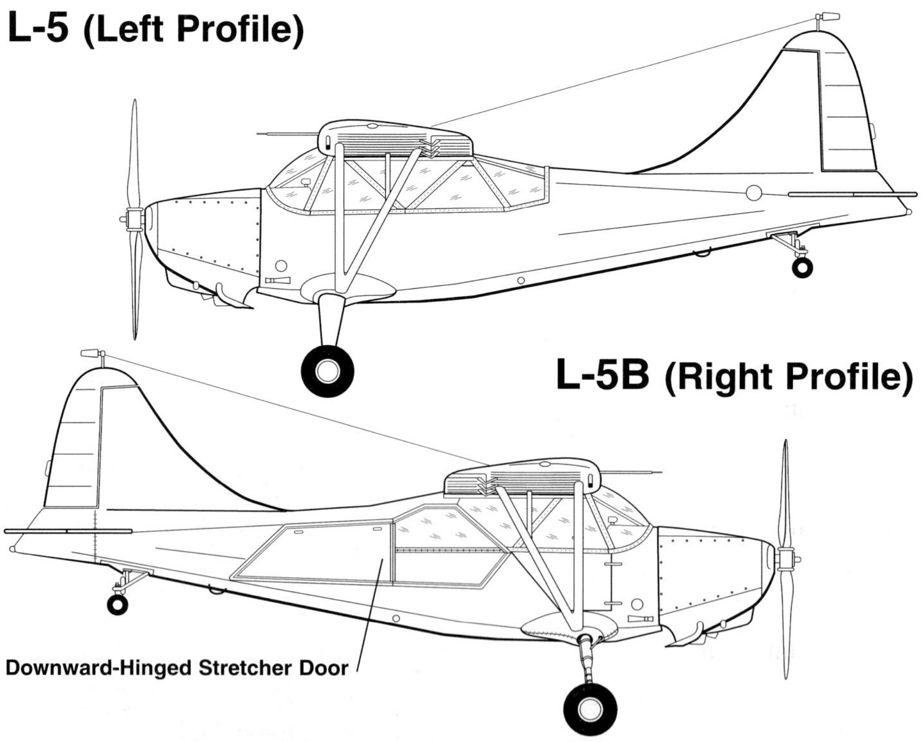

This fair quality image shows a litter-bound US Army soldier is about to be loaded into an L-5B (42-16761) in 1944. The cloth cap-wearing pilot kneeling by the patient's head aided a ground crewman in loading the stretcher into the aircraft. Soon, the patient was flown to a nearby hospital for treatment. Stinson built 730 L-5Bs for the USAAF. (Via Terry Love)

A litter is loaded into an L-5B's aft cockpit, while the right side door remains lowered. The stretcher and its patient were strapped into the Sentinel's cabin to prevent movement during flight. All L-5 variants were equipped with windows in the upper fuselage over the pilot and observer. (Via Terry Love)

A 7th Armored Division, 12th Army Group L-5B (56-K/44-17194) prepares for flight in 1944. The multi-purpose L-5B operated in both the air ambulance and the aerial observer and liaison roles. Helicopters eventually replaced aircraft like the Sentinel in the air ambulance role. (Ken Danielson via Squadron/Signal)

An aircraft mechanic/crew chief poses with his charge, an L-5B (LI-13/44-16906) parked in a grove of fruit trees in a French field. A scantily dressed woman is painted under *The Little Fox* on the cowling. The Sentinel was assigned to C Flight, 173rd LS, 9th Air Force. The 173rd LS primarily operated in the courier role from Orly Aerodrome, Paris. (Frank J. Malmak)

An L-5E (44-17912) from an unidentified unit makes a flight in 1944. The L-5E was basically an L-5C equipped with ailerons that 'drooped' (lowered) in conjunction with the flaps. These 'drooped' ailerons improved short field take-off and landing capabilities. A strap-type step was added to the lower right fuselage. This aided in loading stretchers and cargo. Stinson completed 750 L-5Es from late 1943 until 1944. (US Army)

A Marine Observation Squadron Three (VMO-3) OY-1 (3) is forced down somewhere in the Philippine Islands in 1944. This aircraft came to rest near a ditch and its crew and another Marine took up a defensive fighting position. The broken propeller indicated that the engine was running when the OY-1 impacted with the ground. (Via William E. Davis)

"Sarah," a VMO-3 OY-1, awaits the catapult officer's signal before launching from the escort carrier USS SANGAMON (CVE-26). This occurred during operations off the Philippines in the Fall of 1944. A motion picture camera is mounted on the OY-1's right wing strut support. This camera recorded film of Japanese positions in the objective area. The film was developed after the mission and used to plan subsequent operations. Two Grumman F6F-3 Hellcat fighters of SANGAMON's squadron are spotted behind the OY-1. (National Archives)

A VMO-3 OY-1 makes a Navy turn to port while launching from SANGAMON's flight deck off the Philippines in 1944. The Sentinel has a mottled camouflage pattern on the upper wing and horizontal stabilizer surfaces. The observer's right window is lowered to facilitate a quick exit in case of a water landing. (Real War Photos)

L-5s remained in US Army service until the late 1950s, including service in the Korean War. This L-5E (44-17862) named BUNNY HOPS was assigned to the Eighth Army in 1952. Army Sentinels in Korea flew liaison and Forward Air Control (FAC) missions. FACs marked ground targets for ground attack aircraft. Faster North American T-6 Texans, nicknamed 'Mosquitoes,' soon replaced L-5s in the FAC role. (US Army)

Two Marine mechanics service an OY-1 (BuNo 02779) on Okinawa on 3 April 1945. This was two days after US forces invaded the Japanese-held island. Unusually, a shark mouth is painted on the Sentinel's cowling. The USAAF transferred 306 L-5s to the US Navy, which assigned them to the Marines. (USMC via Dave Ostrowski)

A US Air Force L-5E (44-17609) drops mail to troops manning an M19 Gun Motor Carriage in Korea. The mail was contained in a sack released by the observer from the open left window. This Sentinel is painted overall Aluminum, with a Flat Black anti-glare panel on the upper forward fuselage. (USAF/National Archives)

Wings for Democracy

More World War Two US Aircraft from squadron/signal publications

1026 Curtiss P-40

1036 F6F Hellcat

1043 P-39 Airacobra

1045 P-51 Mustang

1050 B-26 Marauder

1081 F2A Buffalo

1109 P-38 Lightning

1145 F4U Corsair

1191 F4F Wildcat

For more information on squadron/signal books, visit www.squadron.com